FREELANCE PHOTOGRAPHER'S HANDBOOK

T.J. Marino, Dean
Donald Sheff, Director
New York Institute
of
Photography

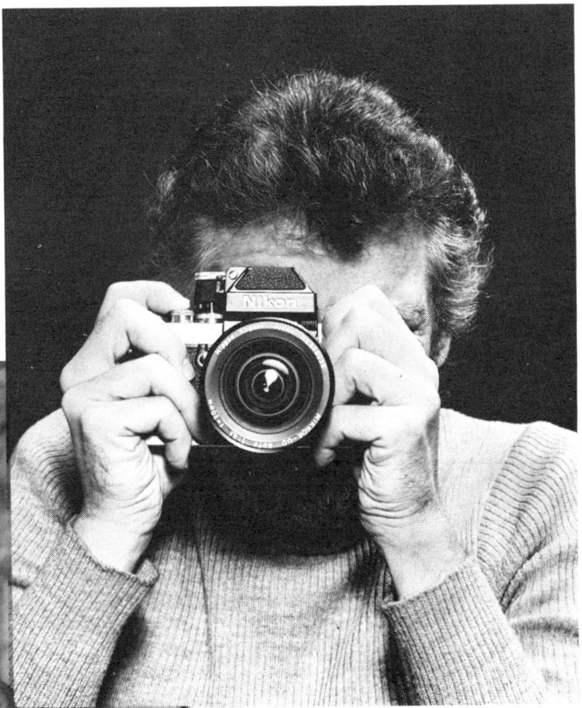

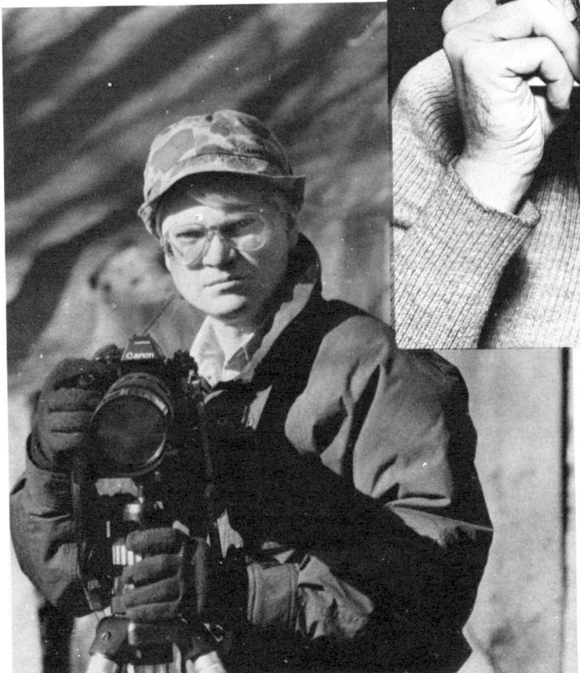

1991 Edition

Printed in U.S.A.

Library of Congress Cataloging in Publication Data

Marino, T.J.
Freelance photographer's handbook.

1. Photography, Commercial — Handbooks, manuals, etc. 2. Photographs — Marketing — Handbooks, manuals, etc. I. Sheff, Donald, joint author. II. Title.
TR690.2.M37 779'.068'8 79-26943
ISBN 0-672-52634-4

Contents

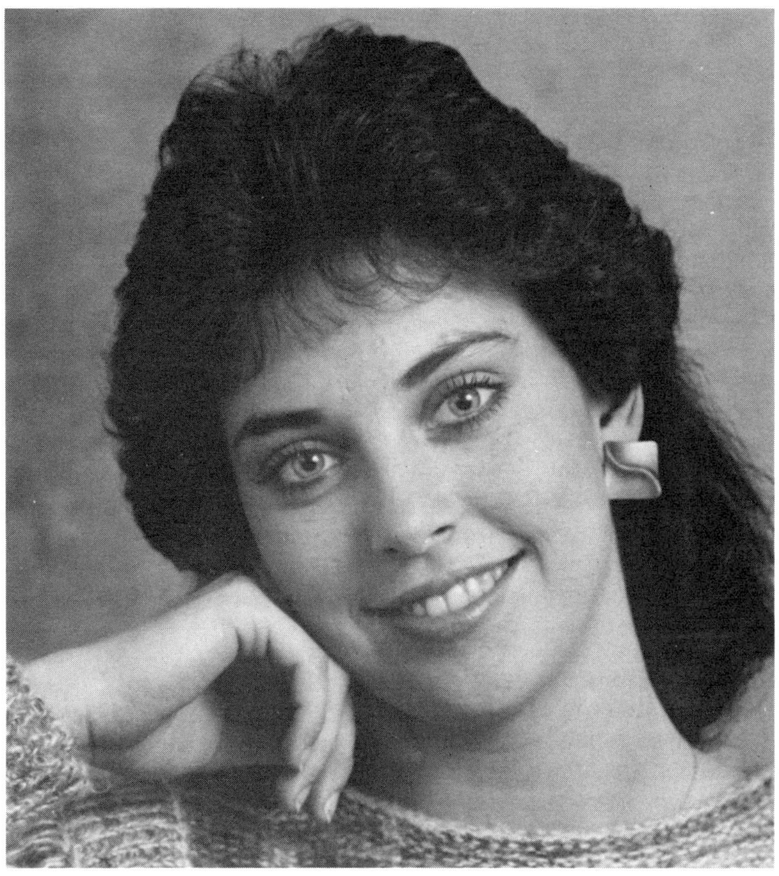

Photo Credit: Lynn J. Upton

Chapter One—Introduction

Chances are, you *love* photography.

But imagine your extra pleasure if you get *paid* for doing what you love. Get paid to have your photographs exhibited. Get paid to have your pictures published in local newspapers or even national magazines. Get paid to have your pictures on file with an international photo agency.

All these things can happen for you as a freelance photographer. And this book is designed to *introduce* you to the most important areas of opportunity that will soon be open to you. We stress the word "introduce" because we recognize that you are just at the start of your quest.

As a beginning student at New York Institute of Photography, you are about to start the training that will enable you to finally succeed as a photographer. Now, you may well think that it will be a long time—perhaps *years*—before you'll be capable of handling the opportunities outlined in this handbook. After all, you've been a camera enthusiast for years—perhaps a lifetime—so you may well expect that it will be many more years—if ever—before you are skilled enough to sell your pictures professionally.

Forget such fears. You won't have to wait "forever." Success is around the corner...if you want it. If you pursue your NYI training with enthusiasm and energy, in just a very few months from now—just a few *months*!—you will be taking photographs of a highly professional character. Pictures you can start to sell to many of the hundreds of buyers listed in this handbook.

What's more, by the time you *finish* your NYI Course—in less than a year—you will have the skills to sell your photographs to just about every professional buyer listed in this handbook. In fact, by the time you finish your NYI Course, your photographs will be superior to those of many so-called "professionals" who are out there right now selling to willing buyers.

Now, you may be wondering, why do we provide you with this handbook now—at the *start* of your NYI Course—when it's real value to you will come later when you are trained? Very frankly, we hope it will inspire you. We hope it will encourage you to work hard during your Course. We hope that once you have seen the "promised land" nothing will stop you from getting to it.

What if you don't intend to pursue a career in photography? What if you're a serious *hobbyist* and simply want to hone your skills to take pictures that you can hang with pride on your living room wall? Pictures that will earn the approval of your loved ones? Pictures that may win a Blue Ribbon in a camera club contest? Fact is, this handbook is as valuable for you as it is for the aspiring professional. Why? Because there's not a hobbyist we know of who wouldn't love to see his or her photographs published in the local paper or magazine. And if they can be *paid* for these pictures in the bargain, so much the better!

So, we're all freelancers at heart. We'd all love to sell some of our pictures even if we don't make this a full-time career.

Of course, for the aspiring *professional* photographer, freelance success is just the starting point for a new career. If you're really serious about a career in photography then—like thousands of NYI graduates before you—you want to move into a *full-time* career when you're ready. Fine. We're going to help you because throughout your NYI Course you are going to receive tips and training in the *business* end of photography. How to get started. How to break in. How to get customers. How to sell!

But that's all later. Now it's time to introduce you to the wonderful world of freelance photography. Realize that you don't have to read this entire handbook right now. Browse through it first. Get an idea of its contents. Then start your NYI Course with Lesson One. As you progress with your NYI training, you will want to refer back to the relevant parts of this handbook that relate to the areas of photography that interest you the most.

Enjoy this handbook. But always remember that it is merely an *introduction* to the areas of opportunity that will open up to you as you progress through your regular NYI training. This handbook covers the *highlights*. The *details* are covered lesson by lesson in your NYI Course.

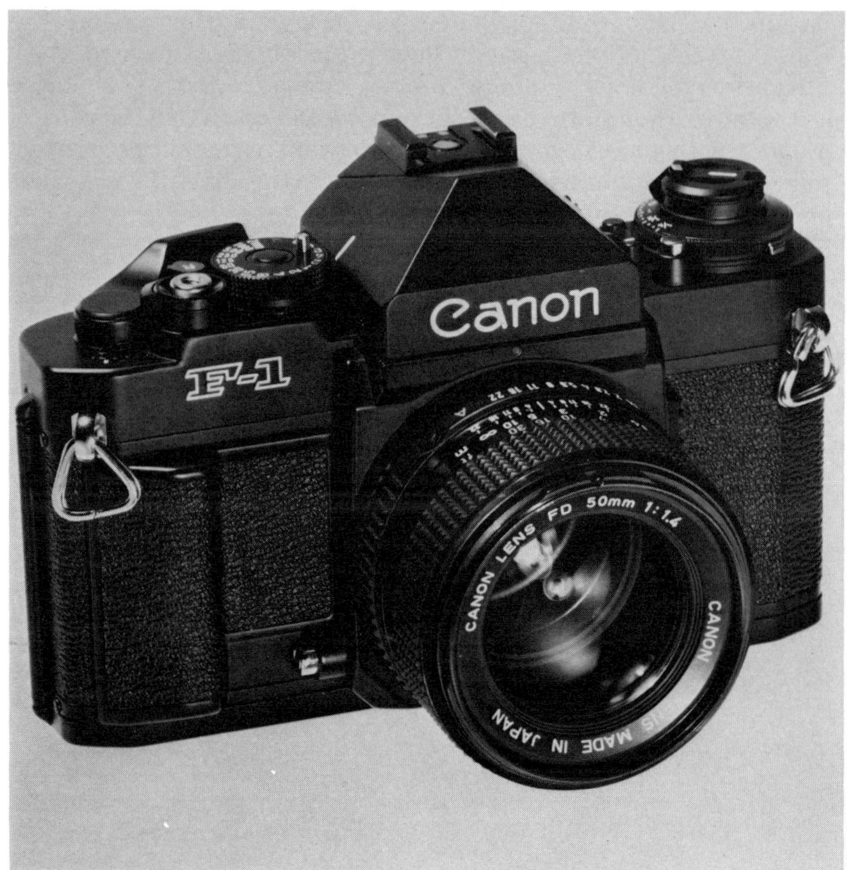

Chapter Two—Basic Equipment

What You Need To Get Started

The typical camera used by most freelancers is a 35mm SLR. Chances are, this is the type of camera you're using too. If you have a camera which is capable of producing a sharp negative, stick with it. It doesn't matter whether your camera is 25-years old or whether it came off the dealer's shelf yesterday. If it produces a negative that makes a clear and sharp 8x10 print, it is more than adequate at the start.

Don't get carried away at the start and run out to buy a whole arsenal of camera bodies, motor drive, wide-angle and telephoto lenses, filters, multiple strobe units and so on. Each of these items is valuable and serves a definite purpose. But at the start *keep it simple.*

The mistake of many amateurs is to concentrate on equipment rather than skill. The successful pro knows that it's his skill that makes the picture, not the fancy doodads on his camera. So don't get wrapped up in the "mine-is-bigger-than-yours" game. Get the few basic pieces of equipment you need, but no more at the start.

What are these basic pieces of equipment? Here's a list of a typical starting kit for a 35mm SLR.

1. *Additional lenses.* In addition to your normal lens, you will find it helpful to also have a moderate wide-angle such as a 35mm or 28mm lens. For example, for photographing the interior of a room or a store, the wide-angle is essential. So, too, you should consider a moderately long lens such as a 105mm or a 135mm. Such a lens is best suited for portraiture and for those situations where approach with a normal lens is not feasible or possible. If you get into photographing children, pets, and people, it could well become your basic lens.

2. *Electronic Flash.* You should have at least one portable strobe unit, preferably two. Automatic-exposure units are most convenient.

3. *Tripod.* You need a good one, light enough to be easily portable, but solid enough to provide a sturdy base for your camera.

4. *Filters.* A few basic filters will come in handy. For black-and-white pictures, you need carry just three basic filters:

Medium yellow— #8
Green — #11
Red — #25

For color photography, you should carry the necessary correction filters that enable you to use your film with alternate light sources. The instruction sheet that comes with your film will tell you the necessary correction filter to use if you shoot with a light source other than the one for which the film is intended.

5. *Carrying Bag.* Your entire set of basic equipment should be packed neatly in a convenient carrying bag so you don't have to lug around a dozen bits and pieces. Safest are the aluminum cases with foam inserts in which you cut out an individual hole for each piece of equipment. These are also the heaviest, so you may prefer a lighter canvas, nylon, or plastic bag. But be sure you can neatly pack your camera, lenses, and accessories so that they don't bang together.

These are the basics. You probably already have most of this equipment so the added cost of getting started should be minimal. As you progress in your freelance work, you may find that you need additional equipment. If the need for a given item is repeated, then you can consider buying it. (You may also consider *renting* it if the need is infrequent.) But, don't buy just for the sake of buying or because you think you might need an exotic piece of equipment "some day."

There's More

Beyond the barest basic equipment we've discussed, lies a galaxy of sophisticated and specialized (and expensive) equipment. Motor drive units that will fire a 36-exposure roll in seconds are part of the arsenal of the advanced freelance. A macro lens and an extreme telephoto (500 to 1000mm) will probably be found in his camera bag, along with an extra camera body and an extreme wide-angle lens such as a 20mm or even a fisheye. Several tripods (one regular and one table-top), several more filters, a soft brush, an exposure meter as insurance against damage to the one in his camera, and a strange variety of nuts, bolts, string, rubber bands, tape, clips and aspirin. If you live near a lake or ocean that offers water sports, then the Nikonos (an underwater camera), may also be required equipment.

After you are working steadily, you may consider building a new camera system with lenses and accessories to extend the versatility of the camera you now own. If you begin to photograph products for magazine or sales brochures, you might consider the advantages of the sophisticated and flexible studio view camera (probably 4x5). Catalog and product shots, especially in color, are enhanced by the larger format. Even more important is the view camera's ability to correct or introduce distortion through its bellows, front and rear tilt, and slides and swings.

Special Equipment and Rentals

It is likely that sometime during the early stages of your photographic career, you will receive an assignment that calls for a piece of equipment that you don't own. Don't panic. Anything under the photographic sun can be rented for a day or a week or longer. If more similar assignments come your way, then some arrangement might be made to have rental costs applied to the ultimate purchase of the particular piece of equipment.

What Should You Buy Now?

Nothing! Don't rush out to buy any equipment you don't already have. Rather...wait. Wait until you've completed the lessons in your NYI Course. In these lessons you'll be shown exactly what you need—and what you *don't* need!—so that you don't waste money on equipment that's showy but not essential.

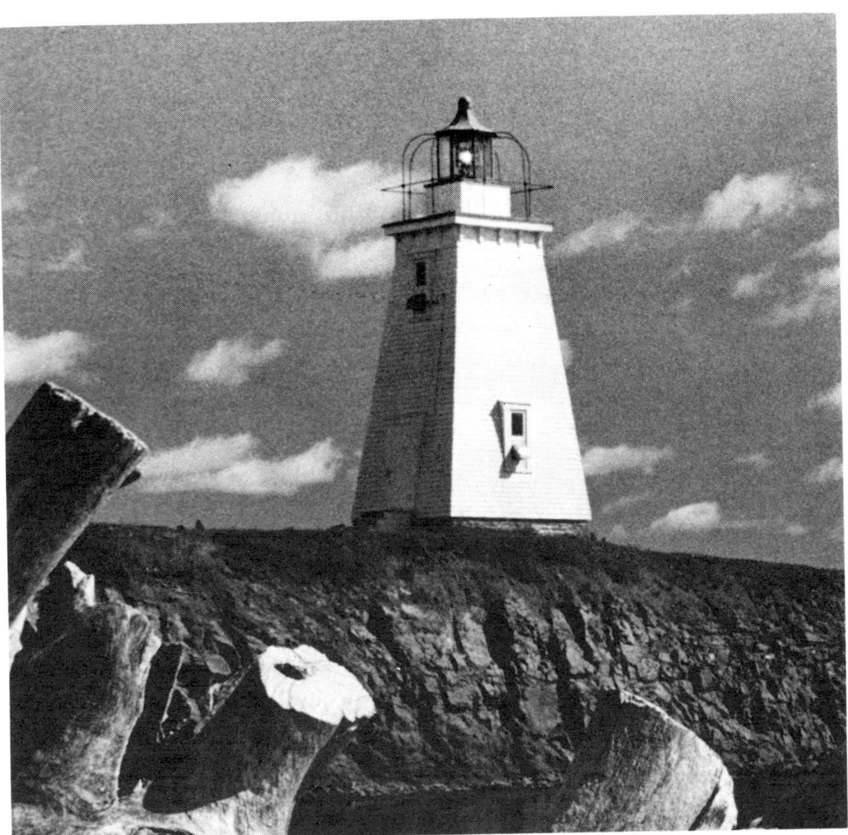

Photo Credit: David Flynn

Chapter Three—What Shall I Photograph?

Evaluate and Analyze The Markets

It's important to know the marketplace. While some publications use only a few pictures a year, others devour photographs in monthly or weekly gulps.

Are you interested in shooting photographs on the farm? Look through the lists in the back of this handbook, and select those publications that request farm pictures or farming scenes. Send for samples of their publications. Offer to pay for them since not all publications will send them free of charge. When they arrive, study them carefully. What is the general format of their photographs? Square or rectangular? One column or two? Black-and-white or color? What type of pictures do they seem to favor? Scenics or the mechanized aspects of farming? Now is the time to learn to be a business man. You're selling a product, so pick the most logical consumer for your wares. While it's nice to concentrate on areas that interest you most, don't let your personal preferences be a straightjacket. Also consider handling those types of work that will be most lucrative because of the availability of the given type of job in your area.

Should You Specialize?

Are you a scuba diver? A sailing enthusiast? A fishing nut? If there is an area in which you are deeply involved and in which you consider yourself an expert, you have a head start on a lot of other photographers. Knowing a subject well and having access to photographs which by their nature are difficult or impossible for the average photographer to obtain, give the specialist a decided advantage over his competitors. Do you live in an area where it snows much of the year and skiers cover the trails? You can specialize! Does the sun shine in your backyard all year round? Many photographers devote much of their time to photographing flowers, trees, and nature subjects. There is a market for *everything*. The freelancer's prime responsibility is to find the market that best suits his or her temperament, interests, *and* locale.

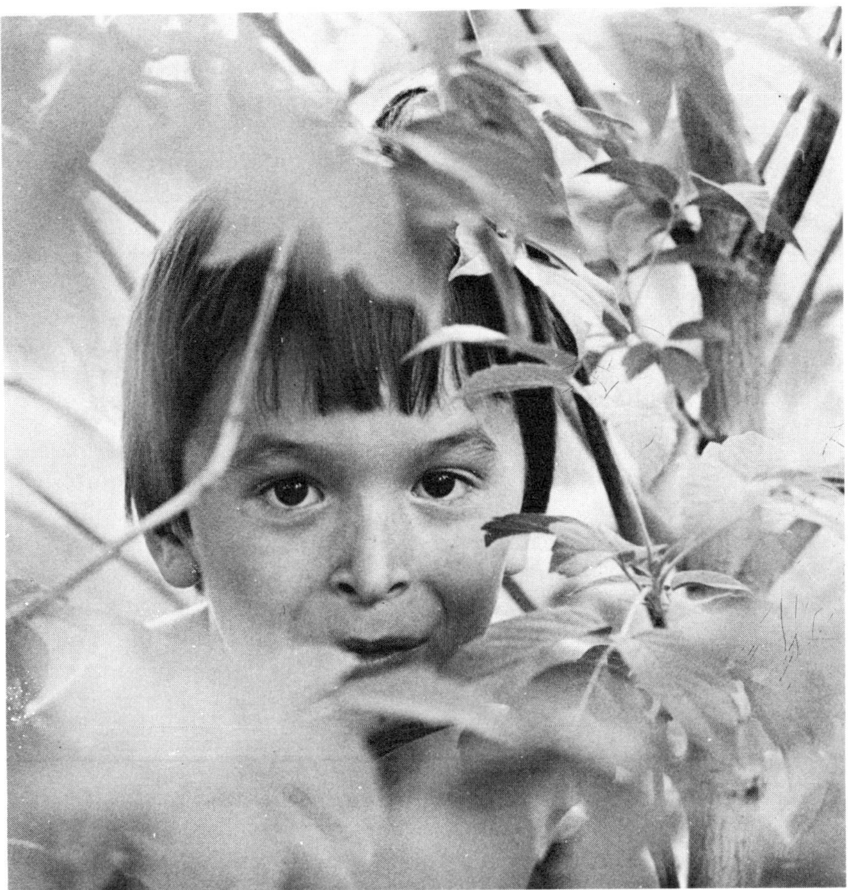

Photo Credit: Bernard W. Robinson

Chapter Four— What Pictures Sell Best?

While the beginning freelancer may seek an obvious and conclusive answer to the question of which pictures sell best, the truth of the matter is that *any* photograph that interested the photographer may also interest someone else. The picture must attract and hold the attention of the viewer. Let us examine the various areas of interest and try to judge for ourselves where we should aim our cameras.

The How-To Picture

It is utterly impossible to open a magazine of any kind and not find a "How-To" article. *How To Build a Darkroom, How To Care For Your Saint Bernard, How To Start a Vegetable Garden, How To Buy a Washer-Dryer* . . . the list goes on forever. The "How-To-Do-It" market probably uses more photographs on a continuing basis than any other market. The reason is simple—every subject under the sun is, or will be, a target for a "How-To" article someday, somewhere.

An article instructing a housewife on the step-by-step procedures for framing a needlepoint may use anywhere from 10 to 30 photographs. Another article may use a dozen or more pictures showing how your air-conditioning unit may be prepared for protection against the winds and snows of winter. A magazine devoted to woodworking may show the hobbyist how to build a simple birdhouse or a picket fence to protect his flower beds. Editors have discovered that if you want to say something to your readers, show them pictures. It's the old grade school game of Show and Tell.

Golfing, skiing, tennis, baseball, and every other sport you can imagine have all been subjects for "How-To" books. In this area, photography has finally been recognized for what it is—the most fantastic medium for education the world has ever known!

A series on "How To Adjust Your Own Carburetor" might require as many as 30 to 50 photographs, beginning with the moment you lift the hood to the time you close it after completing the job. It would show, in consecutive pictures, where the carburetor is, how to disassemble it a screw at a time, how to make adjustments, how to put it back in, how to test it, a description of the various parts and their functions, and finally, before-and-after views showing the carburetor in all its shining, functioning glory! A well-done set of photographs will have every automobile owner in the nation lifting up the hood to familiarize himself with this strange animal. It does not matter that this article was published before. Models change constantly and the series that was printed in last month's magazine may be superseded by changes that took place in the construction of this year's new models. Editors are always on the lookout for sharper photographs, new angles of view, pictures that are different in some way from the ones they have already used. After all, there is virtually nothing *really* original under the sun.

Animals And Pets

The use of animal and pet photographs in both general and specific interest publications probably runs neck and neck with babies and landscapes. They are perennial favorites and the public never tires of well-made pictures of domestic pets or zoo animals. Unfortunately, while simple portraits of wild animals may be used for illustration, domestic animals, because of their familiarity to most households must necessarily be pictured *doing* something. They may be fighting with each other, or sharing the same bowl of food, or carrying a newspaper across the lawn. A cat who has slipped into the bathtub and is being lifted out sopping wet will make a picture. A formal portrait of that same cat would probably not. (Please, don't dunk your cat in the bathtub for the sake of a picture.)

Bird-watchers have an unusual opportunity to make the kind of salable picture that is not easily accessible to most photographers. Photographers who have an affinity for particular animals have a rare opportunity to make unusual and rare pictures that are instantly salable.

Babies And Children

Because they are little people, and mirror-images of ourselves, we all respond to the charming photograph of a child at play, asleep, or getting into unusual situations. Good pictures of children and babies doing things, particularly in normal situations, make sure-fire sellers for illustrations in children's books since children identify easily with other children. Children's photographs are used to sell everything from toiletries to patent medicines. Particularly valuable are photographs of children in different moods. Many an ad has been structured around the "before-and-after" approach. The child may be shown crying or frowning after having supposedly sampled one type of baby food, and then shown smiling in another picture supposedly after having eaten the advertiser's food. This same technique can, of course, be applied to practically anything that has to do with babies. Often, the idea for a picture story may suggest itself during a photographic session with a child. The child may be engaged in an activity that has a logical beginning and ending and may be the kind of story that would be interesting to women's magazines that lean to "homey" material. Since there is probably more money spent on child photographs than in any other area, the thought of being a specialist in the field of child photography certainly bears thinking about. Certainly, it is one of the easiest fields in which to get started since it requires nothing more than a bare minimum of equipment and a love for kids. Doing child portraits in the home is the easiest way of acquiring expertise in the behavior and moods of children. The secret of good children's photographs is an intimate knowledge of their behavior patterns, their responses to sounds, toys, conversation, and tidbits of their favorite food. Parents should be consulted at the time of appointment, and the best time to photograph their child should be determined.

Landscapes And Scenics

The landscape photograph has long been a favorite subject for the freelance photographer. Because a landscape is always there when he is ready to shoot, and because of the timeless quality landscapes possess, the average freelance always has one or more in his portfolio. Landscapes and scenic photographs find a steadily growing market in calendars, magazine covers and postcards. The photographs on picture postcards are probably provided by a photographer who lives in the area. Calendar manufacturers are ever on the lookout for different pictures of the seasons, flower beds, farm scenes, and good views of famous buildings and landmarks. Before you tackle this market, spend some time looking at calendars wherever you go. Remember that just photographing scenery does not automatically produce a landscape. You must be aware of what makes a good landscape photograph. Be aware of the possibilities of various locations. Be selective in your judgments of what view is worth photographing, and have the patience to wait for the correct lighting condition for your chosen view. Don't lose sight of the fact that the inclusion of people in your landscape may limit future sales because as clothing styles and grooming change, the picture will appear quickly dated.

Unusual Hobbies And Special Interests

Do you know someone who builds castles out of matchsticks? Or someone who carves rings out of elephant tusks? Do you have a neighbor who makes shoes by hand just for the fun of it? In every town and every city in the country are people whose unusual hobbies or special interests furnish the necessary material for a series of interesting pictures. Perhaps the Police Chief is an opera buff and during his spare time acts as conductor with the local opera society. Or the barber is a member of the volunteer fire department who leaves his customer sitting in the chair whenever the firebell sounds. Stories of this kind are full of human-interest situations and make excellent picture stories. More important is their sales potential to consumer oriented magazines with large circulations. Anything of general interest has broad sales appeal.

Location Work—Construction—Window Displays

Window display photographs have a ready market. They are salable not only to the store owner, but also to the manufacturer of the products displayed therein. Successful photographs of window displays can be made during the day or after dark depending on the particular display. The best kinds of displays are those that feature the products of a single manufacturer. When too many products from different companies are represented, each of the manufacturers has no interest in your photograph. In this case, the only potential customer might be the store owner himself. In those instances where the display you photograph is a well-known product or the store is one of a chain, your sales potential for that picture immediately increases since the manufacturer and the sales chain may buy your photographs for use in their trade journals.

Construction progress pictures are always in demand. Both the architect and the various building contractors involved in the job are often ready and willing to pay for good photographs taken on a daily or weekly basis. In addition, there are numerous opportunities to make photographs of different construction equipment and products in use.

Whose tractors are on the job? Whose cement is being used? Who is supplying the steel? The glass? As you can see, the possibilities are endless. Just one contact with an architect or builder may give you a steady flow of assignments all year round.

The secret of selling pictures is not to sell your picture once, but to sell it as many times as possible to as many publications as possible.

While this book is primarily geared to the freelance photographer who wants to make money selling his or her photographs, there are also many opportunities to make valuable contacts with people from all walks of life who may represent potential assignments later on.

Weddings, Banquets, Parties

While weddings and banquets are relatively straight shooting jobs where the final product is sold directly to the bride or banquet organizer, the opportunity to earn considerable income exists. Banquet or party pictures can be sold by the hundreds if they are sharp and will printed. Brides need very little coaxing to buy extra prints and extra albums for their parents and close relatives. Perhaps even more important than the income derived from these assignments is the fact that you have the opportunity to pass out *hundreds* of business cards and make the kind of contacts that represent future business. In any large gathering it is safe to say that you may find a lawyer, an architect, a manufacturer, or a restaurant owner. Any and all of these people—to name just a few—can use your services at one time or another.

It is a sound business idea when shooting a particularly attractive wedding couple to try to get a model release signed if you think some of the photographs might have a chance at being published in consumer magazines which are women-oriented. A particularly poignant moment in the ceremony may contain just the kind of human interest that will lift the photograph out of the commonplace and into the sphere of universality—where *anyone* will enjoy looking at the picture. This is the kind of picture that an editor will buy.

In your efforts to secure a model release, don't be obvious! Mention that you might have an opportunity to have a picture or two published some time in the future. This will certainly flatter the bride and make your job easier. You might, if it "feels" right, offer an extra 11x14 print or some other inducement, but don't push!

Legal Photography

Because of the nature of photographs made for evidence, most work of this kind is done on location. It represents an ideal opportunity for the freelance to work under a variety of conditions and cover a broad range of subjects. Photographs for use in the courtroom must necessarily be absolutely sharp and clear. Angles of view should coincide with those of eyewitnesses, if any. A photograph of a broken stair need not be artistic—just clear! Tire marks in the roadway should be photographed at an angle that shows them clearly. Look for the best lighting condition, which will usually be from a 45- or 90-degree angle. Take both close-up views and views showing related environment or surroundings.

Should legal photography interest you, start by contacting every lawyer and police chief in your area and offer to show samples of your work. While many lawyers and police departments make use of Polaroid cameras for this kind of work, the truth of the matter is that most of the photographs they produce are entirely inadequate compared to a clean, sharp, professionally made print. Your job is to convince them that you can do the job better!

In your NYI Course you will receive tips and training on all these areas. So, don't rush out now to try to sell your favorite picture of the Fourth of July parade. Wait until you've completed the lesson on Photojournalism—and every other appropriate lesson—to make sure that your ''favorite picture'' is really up to the professional standards you are going to be able to attain shortly.

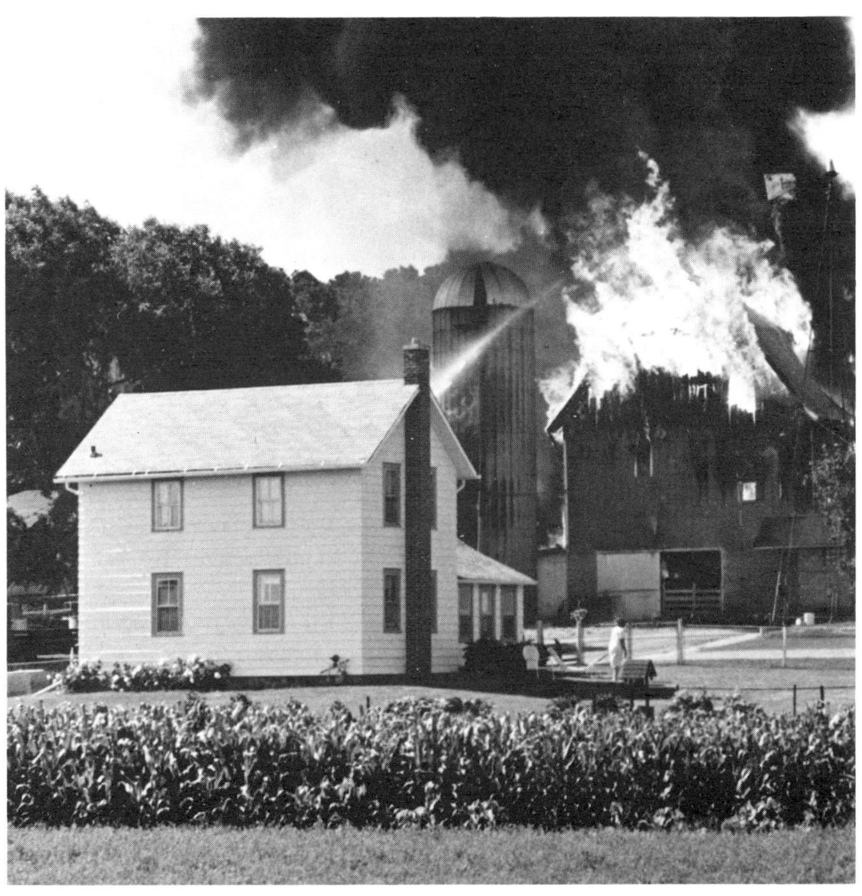

Photo Credit: James B. Kennedy

Chapter Five— Press Photography

Spot News Photography

News is happening all the time all around you. Whether it's a sudden accident or the July 4th parade, it's news. And a good photograph may be used by the local newspaper or television station. While the bigger papers and stations have their own staff photographers, they can't be *everywhere.* If you are alert and move fast, you can often beat them to the scene of a sudden unexpected occurrence.

Monitor Police and Fire Radio

If you are serious about news photography, you may want to invest in a *scanning* radio receiver that continuously scans the different police and fire department frequencies, locking onto those that are transmitting at the moment. Note that a mobile police receiver in your car is illegal.

When you hear an accident or fire reported over one of the channels, get going! Have your camera bag ever ready, cameras loaded, strobes charged, and your Press Card handy if you have one. Also be ready with the phone numbers of local newspapers and television stations. And have some dimes handy.

Press Cards

If you get to the scene of an emergency fast, you won't be bothered by police cordons. You can get your pictures fast, and get out. If you are not there soon enough, however, you may find that the police or firemen have blocked off the area surrounding an accident or fire. To get through, you have a number of approaches.

Best of all is a *press card.* This is an *official* card issued by the local police department to bona-fide members of the working press. Usually it is issued only to staff photographers of the local papers or stations or representatives of syndicates such as Associated Press, AP. Inquire at your local police headquarters as to procedures in your community. With an official press card, you can get through almost any police lines.

If you are not yet entitled to an official press card—and you probably aren't—don't despair. You are not going to be left out in the cold. Because you are a student of the New York Institute of Photography, you are going to receive as part of your Course your own personal Press Card indicating that you are an Official Photographer for *NYI Photoworld Magazine*—our school publication. Along with it you will receive complete instructions on how to use this "courtesy card" to obtain the greatest possible cooperation from local police and other authorities.

Will your *NYI Photoworld Press Card* really help you get into "press-only" areas? Recently, one NYI student was admitted by the Secret Service to photograph the President when he arrived at a local Air Force base. It works, if you use it properly. And you'll learn all about this in your Course.

Getting The Pictures

While you are enroute to the scene of the occurrence, plan ahead.

Plan where to park your car so that you can most easily get to the scene *and* most easily get away from it so that you can rush your film back to your dark room. Park far enough away so you won't hinder emergency crews. Check the direction of the sun and ponder how it can be best used. If you're going to a fire, check the wind direction, considering how it will affect the smoke.

Check nearby buildings to see if there are any potential vantage points for your shooting.

When you get to the scene, size up the situation as fast as you can. We won't review all the fundamentals of news photography here, but try to shoot pictures that clearly and simply show *what* is happening, *who* is involved, *where* it is happening, and *what's* going on.

Usually your first shots are the best. Concentrate on the victim or structure that's the subject of the event. After you've got shots that clearly show the occurrence, shoot "background" pictures of the police or firemen in action, their equipment at the scene, the reactions of bystanders or witnesses.

Most important, write down the facts. Get the names of the victims. The address of the location. The names, where possible, of the personnel or bystanders you've photographed. Within the limits of time, be your own reporter. Get the information fast. Get it accurately. Get it in writing. And . . . get out!

Calling Your Market

When you have all the shots—and the related information—get to the nearest phone and call the local newspapers and television stations. (Remember, you arrived on the scene prepared with all their phone numbers and with change to make the calls.) Ask for the *picture desk* or *news desk.* Tell them what you have. If they are interested, they will ask you to either come right in with your raw film so that their lab can print it—or, if time is not too pressured, they may ask you to quickly develop and print your film and deliver the prints to them.

Don't sell the same print to more than one paper or station. But, you are free to sell *different* pictures to different news media.

If you are instructed to deliver your film or prints to a distant place by messenger, bus, train, or plane, be sure to write down the name of the carrier, the correct flight number or schedule number, the name or badge number of the messenger, and any other pertinent details, *plus* the name and precise address of the person to whom your material is being sent. As soon as it's on its way, call or wire the person it's going to, giving him all the details on how it was sent, when and where it will arrive in his city, and so on.

Crashing The Wire Services

If spot news photographs interest you, and you have sold an occasional photograph from time to time, the idea of becoming a "stringer" with one of the major wire services may appeal to you. A stringer is a freelance photographer who supplies pictures from areas of the country that are not normally covered by the regular staff of a TV station or wire service (such as UPI and AP). Becoming a stringer is achieved by the steady submission of high-quality and timely pictures and stories from those remote locations not covered by the TV or wire service staffs. In other words, you must bring your skills to someone's attention. The most common and workable method is to establish a relationship with a newspaper in your area which subscribes to UPI or AP services. They will bring unusual or particularly interesting pictures and stories to the attention of the TV stations and wire services, who may, after a while, express an interest in *you.* When they do, you will probably be *asked* to provide news coverage of interesting events and happenings from your area. Most stringers are retained on a small monthly fee basis withh additional payment being made for stories they cover.

Television Also Offers Opportunities

How often have you seen stills of events in outlying communities or locales flash across your television screen? These are more often than not made by stringers who reside in areas too remote for a television station to want to send a full-time staff member. One of the best ways to break into this field is to send some of your best scenics to the nearest television station with a short note stating that you are available for work in your area should the need arise—naturally, including your phone number and address.

Market Guide—Press Photography

Consult your local, regional, and urban newspapers. In addition, review the following directories and guides available at your public library or bookstores:

American Society of Journalists and Authors
Directory of Professional Writers
1501 Broadway, Suite 1907
New York, NY. 10036

A.P.I. (Associated Press International)
50 Rockefeller Plaza
New York, NY. 10020

Contact Book for the Entertainment Industry
Celebrity Service, Inc.
171 W. 57th Street
New York, NY. 10019

Register of the Public Relations Society of America
845 Third Avenue
New York, NY. 10022

Television Contacts
Larimi Communication, Ltd.
151 50th Street
New York, NY. 10022

Ulrich's International Periodicals Directory
R.R. Bowker
1180 Avenue of the Americas
New York, NY. 10036

U.P.I. (United Press International)
48 East 21st Street
New York, NY. 10010

Where and How to Sell Your Pictures
Amphoto (American Photographic Book Publishing Co.)
1515 Broadway
New York, NY. 10036

The World Almanac
Newspaper Enterprise Association
200 Park Avenue
New York, NY. 10017

World Travel Directory
Ziff-Davis Publishing Co.
1 Park Avenue, Room 1011
New York, NY. 10016

Writer's and Photographer's Guide
Clarence House Publishers
2115 Van Ness Avenue
San Francisco, CA. 94109

Writer's and Photographer's Guide to Newspaper Markets
Helm Publishing
Box 10512
Evansville, IN. 47734

A Writer's Guide to Chicago-Area Publishers
Writer's Guide Publications
Gabriel House, Inc.
9329 Crawford Avenue
Evanston, IL. 60203

Writer's Guide to West Coast Publishing
Hwong Publishing
10353 Los Alamitos Blvd.
Los Alamitos, CA. 90720

Writer's Market
9933 Alliance Road
Cincinnati, OH. 45242

Working Press of the Nation
Internal Publications Directory
National Research Bureau
424 N. 3rd Street
Burlington, IA. 52601

- Vol 1. Newspapers
- Vol 2. Magazines
- Vol 3. TV and Radio
- Vol 4. Feature Writers and Photographers
- Vol 5. Internal Publications

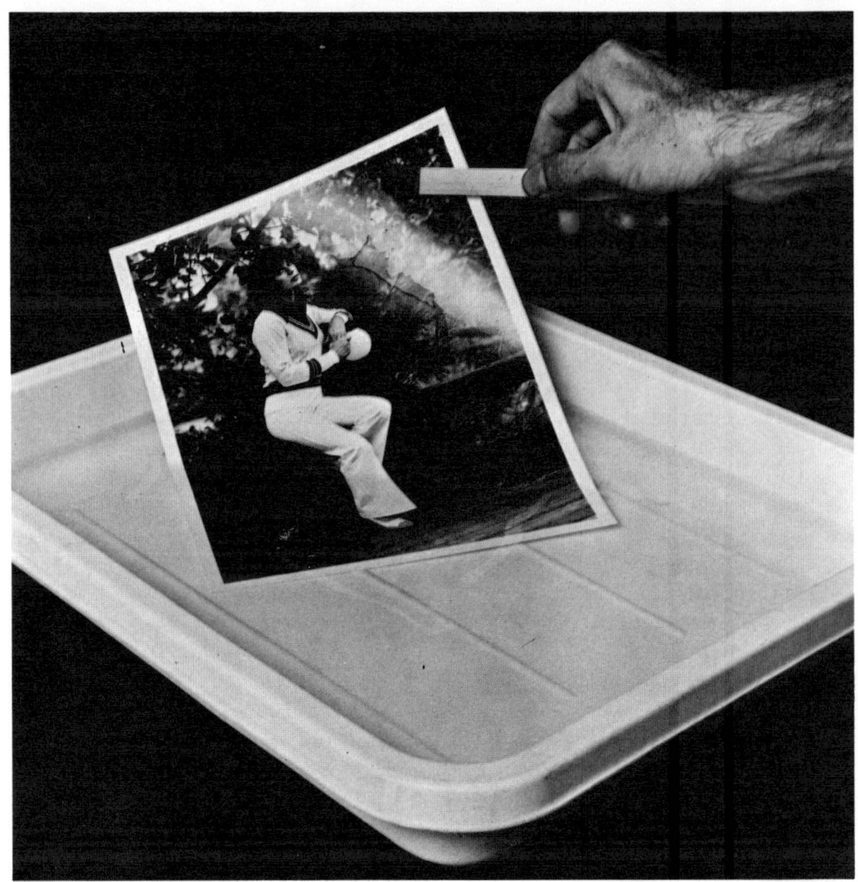

Chapter Seven— After You Have Taken The Photograph

How To Prepare Prints For Submission

Whether the finished print has been made in your own darkroom or a commercial lab, a high standard of quality is a necessity. All prints should have a good tonal range and be free from spots and scratches. The generally accepted print is 8x10 inches, glossy, double-weight. Avoid sending pictures that are either too small or too large. 8x10 is *standard* throughout the photographic world since it is small enough for easy filing and mailing, and yet large enough for easy viewing.

Captions

All photographs should have the name and address of the photographer stamped on the back. Caption information should be typed on a separate sheet of paper (use the lower half of the sheet). This caption information is then affixed to the back of the print with photographic rubber cement or masking tape. (Do not use Scotch brand tape; it's bad for photographs.) Fold the bottom half of the paper containing the information over the face of the print. When the editor looks at your photograph he should be able to fold down the part of the paper containing the information, and see both the photograph and the caption material at the same time.

Captions For Slides

While there are several methods for furnishing caption information when submitting slides, the most accepted method is to type caption information on a separate sheet of paper. Number each caption to correspond to its related slide. Don't forget to number the slide! While in some isolated cases, strips may be affixed to slide mounts, the required information usually takes more space than the slide mount affords. Since the bulk of freelance slide submissions are 35mm, the use of a separate sheet for caption material is by far the most practical method.

Captions—The "Five W's"

Who? What? When? Where? Why? Try to include the answers to these Five W's. Perhaps "flowers in the fields" would not respond to the query "Who?", yet every effort should be made to furnish complete and detailed information for every photograph you submit. If you think something is not important enough to include in the caption information, submit it anyway! Let the editor be the judge of whether it's useful or not. Remember, you *can't* give him too much information —but the danger does exist that you may not give him enough!

How To Package Your Submissions

When you mail your prints or transparencies to a potential buyer, impress him with the fact that you know your job. Don't send sloppily packaged work. You may lose the sale before he even opens the package. Depending upon what you are mailing, there are professional materials available for all types of submissions, as follows.

Mailing Envelopes

Your dealer will be able to supply you with standard mailing envelopes for your 8x10 prints. These are larger all around than the actual size of the print itself, and come in 9x12 or 10x13 sizes. They contain two heavy cardboard inserts and are clearly imprinted with the legend: "PHOTOGRAPHS—DO NOT BEND." If you have difficulty locating envelopes with cardboard inserts, then simply buy the plain imprinted envelopes and cut *clean* cardboard fillers from boxes you can obtain at the corner grocery. While some photographers use the envelope or box in which photographic paper is packaged, it is not nearly so professional or impressive as the envelope made especially for mailing prints.

Insert your print (or prints) between the two cardboard inserts, affix rubber bands which snap over opposite corners of your cardboard sandwich (two rubber bands required), and you're ready for mailing.

The Mailing Case

By far the most satisfactory method of mailing large quantities of prints is through the use of fibreboard mailing cases with straps, available at most photo dealers and art supply houses. These cases are sturdy and durable and will withstand the roughest kind of abuse. They are provided with a removable return address card and space for postage. Upon completing his viewing of your photographs, the editor merely reverses the stamped-addressed card and the package is on its way back to you. This type of mailing case is definitely recommended for mailing prints that are rare or are difficult to print again. Be sure to affix stamps to your return package or envelope. Nothing is more annoying to a picture editor than to open an envelope and have loose stamps fall out. Avoid the use of adhesives, staples or clips that may abrade or damage photographs or slides in the package.

Postage

For occasional mailings of several prints, first-class mail is recommended. Your prints will arrive in the shortest possible time and not be subject to the uncertain delivery schedule of third-class rates. If you are submitting on a speculation basis, editors take a dim view of having to pay postage to return your pictures to you. You will get prompt and courteous replies if you enclose with your photographs a stamped self-addressed envelope that has affixed to it the proper amount of postage for its return to you. This can make a real difference as to how the picture editors welcome your current submission and your future ones!

Submitting Photographs In Person

If you are fortunate enough to live within traveling distance of the publication to which you are submitting work, you may consider the desirability of making a personal call instead of using the mails. There are both advantages and disadvantages to this method. The obvious advantage is in being able to discuss your work with the picture buyer, and perhaps ascertain his needs for the future. The drawback is that editors simply do not have the time to sit down and chat with every photographer who has prints to sell. Handling material through the mail gives him the opportunity to look at pictures leisurely within the framework of his own schedule. Play this one carefully. If you *do* decide to call an editor and he gives the *slightest* clue that your coming in person might be an imposition—don't push. Offer to send the material in the mail. Picture editors are really nice people for the most part, and are continually pressed for time. They can examine submissions-by-mail from a dozen photographers in the quiet of their office in much less time than it takes to interview even one.

Should You Write A Letter First?

Avoid unnecessary letter writing. If you do write to a publication, you should have something specific to talk about. If the letter concerns the photographs you are submitting, it should simply indicate that the pictures being offered for sale are at the publication's prevailing rates. Do *not* ask how much they pay. Publications have standard rates for each picture they buy *or* a rate based upon the size of the space given to the picture when it is published—such as full-page, half-page, etc. Since the rates they pay are usually included in their market listings, it is the sign of an amateur to ask payment rates.

If you have something significant to say about the pictures you are submitting, then by all means write a letter. You may wish to point out that a particular picture in the group has already been published elsewhere, or that a model release is available for pictures containing likenesses of people. This information, incidentally, can easily be stamped on the back of the print to make the editor's life easier. If you submit a photograph that is special in some way, you may indicate that you would like to discuss the type of rights you are willing to sell.

A market listing will often contain the phrase "Query first." This is an invitation to write a letter *before* you submit prints or slides. Describe briefly what you are offering for sale—nothing more! In the absence of a specific person listed as picture editor, simply address your letter to *Picture Buyer.* It will find its way to the proper department and proper person. Since there is frequent turnover in personnel, the guy or gal whose name is listed today may be gone tomorrow, but the publication will always have a Picture Buyer or Picture Editor!

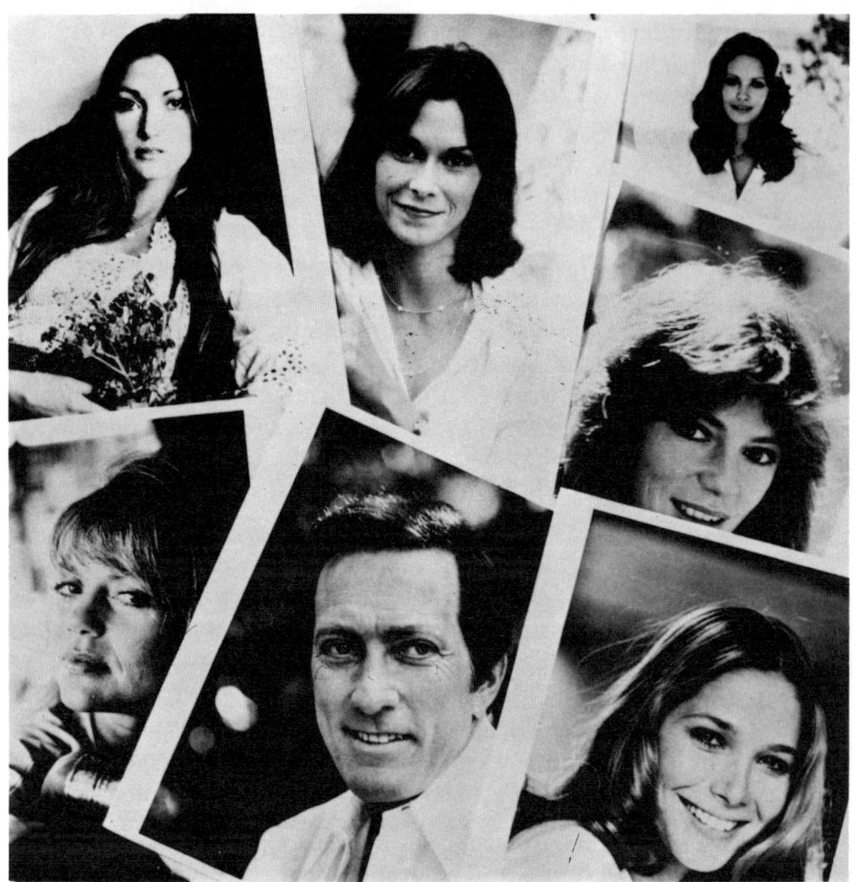

Chapter Seven—
Picture Agencies

The Stock Photograph

A stock photograph is any picture that belongs to the photographer and whose sale is handled by a picture agency or "stock house."

This type of picture can be sold over and over again, as long as the photographer sells what is called *one-time publication* rights. This simply means that the buyer of the photograph is purchasing the right to reproduce it once, and once only. The photographer (or his agency) may then sell the same picture to another publication under the same *one-time* publication rights. Note that the photographer has made two sales, *but still owns the rights to the picture.* This is the key to continued income from the sale of your pictures. Only under unusual circumstances will the photographer or his agency sell a picture outright. Outright sales of original material naturally command much higher prices than one-time publication rights. The different types of publication rights and the correct way to assign these rights will be discussed in a separate chapter.

Any budding freelance has large quantities of 8x10 prints that are sitting around in boxes. The day comes when he considers entering the field in a serious way. He separates his prints by category and discovers that he has hundreds of salable photographs. He compares what he has photographed with the reproductions in various magazines and realizes his photographs are as good or *better* than most of the ones he sees. What's the next step?

First, a comprehensive breakdown of pictures by *specific* subjects. Picture agencies file photographs by major subject headings within which there are subdivisions. For instance, the category BOATS may be subdivided into Small, Medium, Large, Sail, Tug, Yacht, Liner, etc. CHILDREN (a large category), may be subdivided into *At Play, Asleep, With Toys, With Adults, Girls, Boys,* etc. BE SPECIFIC. The buyer will love you for it.

Making The First Contact

Consult the market listing at the end of this chapter, headed *Picture Agencies.* Choose one agency and write a short note outlining *exactly* what you have. If you have a specific area in which you excel (farm pictures, industrial shots, etc.) mention this in your letter. Tell the buyer you would like to send in your prints or transparencies with a view to being signed on by the agency. Most agencies welcome new photographers with a fresh viewpoint, and pay prompt attention to submissions. *Do not send unsolicited photographs.*

The Agency's Function

Picture agencies are in business to sell pictures. If they sign you on they expect you to produce on a regular basis. If you have the idea that you're going to send them a dozen photographs and then sit back and relax—forget it! The picture agency is not for you. But if you are the kind of photographer who grabs his bag and goes out shooting every spare moment, the chances are that in a very short while you will amass a respectable collection for the agency's files. The more of your pictures they have, the greater your chances for a sale.

The Advantages Of Working Through An Agency

While most freelance photographers always find the time to take photographs, they seldom find the time to market their pictures. Selling takes both time and expertise. The agency frees the photographer from the burden of selling. Once the photographer has established himself with an agency, he may be told that certain types of pictures are in demand, and thus be able to direct his efforts to a particular subject or theme. An active picture agency may receive hundreds of calls a week requesting specific types of photographs. A call may come in stating that, "We need a picture of a lady working in her vegetable garden." The agency will look in its *Gardening* file; in its *Vegetables* file (if it has one); and then probably look in its *Women—Outdoors* file, in an effort to come up with a picture that will fill the client's request. Suitable pictures are mailed to the client who will either return them with a note that they are unsuitable, or keep the one or two he needs for publication and return the rest. After using the desired photographs, he returns them, too. If the picture of the lady working in the garden was one of yours—you've made a sale!

Keep Records

There is nothing unethical about sending your pictures to more than one agency. The important thing is that you know every minute exactly who has what! There are, however, pitfalls inherent in sending the *same* material to more than one agency. Since agencies set different fees for the pictures they sell, there always exists the danger that your photograph may be offered for sale to the same buyer by two different agencies. At two different prices! While this may make the buyer happy since he will naturally buy the picture at the lower rate, the second agency may take a dim view of your business ethics and refuse to stock your pictures. While the photographer in most cases has no control over prices charged for pictures, he may, when the same pictures are on file with two or more agencies, attempt to set a minimum sale price. The best policy is to send different photographs to different agencies.

Be Patient

Once you have successfully placed some of your pictures with a stock photo agency, avoid the tendency to wait for the postman every morning in the expectation of receiving checks by return mail. Give the agencies time to do their work. Your pictures may go out a dozen times over the course of a year and never be quite what the buyer is looking for. Or, they may be sold on their very first trip. More likely, the first condition will apply. If the agency accepted your pictures for their files *they will sell.* Just be patient.

Finally—Follow The Rules

If the listing indicates that "2¼x2¼ or larger transparencies" are required, don't send 35mm. If the listing specifies that a stamped self-addressed envelope is required (SASE), be sure to send one or you may not receive a reply to your letter of inquiry. Many agencies will specify the length of time in which they will reply to a picture submission. Some agencies will only send picture requirements (current needs) to those photographers they deem "qualified" after an evaluation of their photographs. If they feel that you have potential, they will send you a sheet listing their current need —which is, in effect, an invitation to shoot on speculation for them. It's a step in the right direction!

Some agencies request that your name and address *not* appear on the back of the print or slide you submit. There's a good reason for this. They are wary of the fact that a prospective buyer may circumvent them and try to buy pictures directly from the photographer at a much lower rate. They also do *not* want the photographer to know who the client is since unscrupulous photographers may attempt to deal with the client directly and thus avoid the agency's rightfully earned fees. *Follow the rules.*

The Agency Contract

Most well-known agencies are thoroughly honest, and their contract forms are standards for the industry. There should be no hesitation on the part of the photographer to sign a standard agency form. This does *not* mean that you shouldn't read it before you sign it. But don't expect to revolutionize industry standards.

The Agency Commission

The average agency commission is 50% of the sale price. Since they contact markets daily and reach into areas totally unknown to the photographer, this fee of 50% is really quite fair. If the average photographer gets irked from time to time because half of every dollar earned goes to the agency, then consider this: For every buyer you can dig up, the agency will contact a hundred. For every picture you may sell, the agency will sell ten or more. They expend enormous sums in overhead costs for salaries, rents, mailing costs and phone bills. Remember, selling pictures continuously is more difficult than taking them!

Types Of Agencies

While a large number of agencies will handle pictures of any subject, many tend to specialize in particular kinds of photographs. Some agencies that handle historical or theatrical or sporting photographs from the past will not usually buy from a freelance since their stock files are built up through the acquisition of estates, collections, and discovery of heretofore unpublished photographs. Both the Bettman Archive and Culver Pictures (in New York City) are examples of this type of agency.

The first job of the freelance then, is to research his market guide thoroughly and determine what agencies would be the most likely to buy the sort of photographs he produces. For instance, the *Animals, Animals Agency* and the *Outdoor Photographers League* all specialize in pictures of flora, fauna, and other wildlife pictures. The *Black Star* agency handles almost anything under the sun provided it's *good.* Their prime interest is more in the quality of what you have to offer than in quantity (although more quantity helps produce more dollars). *Magnum* has a "stable" of top photographers such as Ernst Haas, Henri Cartier-Bresson, and Bruce Davidson. These photographers will produce, on assignment, the special and urgent needs of the agency. *Black Star* also has its own "stable." Buyers of pictures will often contact either of these agencies with a request for a series of photographs whose content is specifically detailed. There *is* room, however, at either agency for exceptional freelance material. Don't send them pictures of the family pet taking a nap—they're not interested! They are interested in top-quality, *unusual* photographs.

The General Stock-Photo Agency

While agencies that specialize are an important part of the overall stock agency field, by far the majority of picture agencies term themselves "general." This means that if a buyer were to enter their premises and say, "I'd like to see what you have in the way of sailboats, shepherding, and coal-mining," the agency could probably place in front of the prospective buyer a stack of prints or transparencies in each of these categories. While general agencies handle a wide range of subjects, they rarely involve themselves with highly specialized material such as diamond-cutting or cane weaving, leaving those areas to the specialist agencies. Market listings are often highly detailed as to the specific wants of each agency, whether they be specialized or general. *Study your market.*

Keep Your Submissions Current

Today's happening is tomorrow's agency requirement. The world is changing rapidly and with it, views and areas of focus. When the age of protest passed, a new era was ushered in, that of the protectors of the environment. The word "ecology" found its way into our everyday conversation and people became increasingly aware of the need to marshall their forces against the rape of nature and the destruction of our natural resources. Currently, there are not *enough* good pictures to fill the need in this area.

Your television set is a good barometer of what occupies the nation's attention these days. Sports have captured a larger and larger share of our attention due to the increased leisure time of most Americans. There is always a good market for excellent sports photographs of all kinds. Politicians and statesmen have concerned themselves more and more with our urban ghettos and disenchanted and disadvantaged youth. Essays in this area (especially with accompanying text) always find a market. Television, particularly, is using still photographs in ever-increasing numbers as back-up material for their newscasts. In some instances, still photographs have been the sole material used in TV documentary and special presentations. But the pictures usually are very current.

To summarize, the fact that a photographer has pictures in one or two agency files is not an indication that he can now simply sit back and wait for sales. Photographs *do* become outdated due to changing styles and fashions so that a continuous and *current* flow of pictures is essential to building the kind of stock photo file that will be earning money on a steady basis.

NYI may be able to help you here if your work is truly outstanding. We have made special arrangements with the *Freelance Photographer's Guild*—one of the largest photo agencies in the world—to bring to their attention the work of our truly outstanding students. Realize, however, that we do this only for the rare ''genius.'' We will not honor any request that emanates from the student himself. The decision must emanate from and be independently agreed upon by the faculty.

Even if you don't qualify for this rare honor, however, you will find that there are dozens of other photo agencies that will be interested in your work if it is good, as indicated in the following lists:

Market Guide — Picture Agencies

Listed below are two directories available to help you target specific markets of interest. Following is a list of individual stock agencies, or picture agencies, which will buy photos from freelance photographers.

Directories

Photographer's Market (Annual)
Writer's Digest Books
9933 Alliance Rd.
Cincinnati, OH. 45242

Stock Photo & Assignment Source Book
R.S. Persky, Publisher
Photographic Arts Center
127 E. 59th St.
New York, NY. 10022

Stock Photo Agencies

Afterimage, Inc.
3807 Wilshire Blvd.
Suite 2550
Los Angeles, CA. 90010

Air Pixies
515 Madison Avenue
New York, NY. 10022
(212) 489-9828

Alaska Photo
1530 Westlake Avenue N.
Seattle, WA. 98109
(206) 282-8116

American Stock Photos
6842 Sunset Blvd.
Hollywood, CA. 90028
(213) 469-3908

Amwest Picture Agency
1595 S. University
Denver, CO. 80210
(303) 777-2770

Animals Animals Enterprises
203 W. 81st Street
New York, NY. 10024
(212) 580-9595

Aperture Photobank, Inc.
1530 Westlake Avenue N.
Seattle, WA. 98109

Art Resource
65 Bleecker Street, 9th Floor
New York, NY. 10012

Bettman Archive, Inc.
136 E. 57th Street
New York, N.Y. 10022

Black Star Publishing Co.
450 Park Avenue S.
New York, NY. 10016

Camerique
1701 Shippack Pike
Box 175
Blue Bell, PA. 19422

Candida Photos
4711 W. Byron Street
Chicago, IL. 60641
(312) 736-5544

Celebrity Photos, Unlimited
Box 166
Bartow, FL. 33830
(813) 533-6845

Bruce Coleman, Inc.
381 5th Avenue
New York, NY. 10016
(212) 683-5227

Community Features
Box 1062
Berkeley, CA. 94701

Compu/Pix/Rental
21822 Sherman Way
Canoga Park, CA. 91303
(213) 888-9270

Culver Pictures
660 1st Avenue
New York, NY. 10016

Cyr Color Photo Agency
PO Box 2148
Norwalk, CT. 06856
(203) 838-8230

Design Photographers International
521 Madison Avenue
New York, NY. 10022

Devaney Stock Photos
122 E. 42nd Street
New York, NY. 10017
(212) 767-6900

Earth Images
Box 10352
Bainbridge Island, WA. 98110
(206) 842-7793

Eastern Stock Photos
1637 Lake Road
Youngstown, NY. 14174

First Foto Bank, Inc.
304 E. Diamond Avenue
Gaithersburg, MD. 20877
(301) 670-0299

Florida Image File
222 2nd Street N.
St. Petersburg, FL. 33701
(813) 894-8433

Franklin Photo Agency
85 James Otis Avenue
Centerville, MA. 02632
(603) 889-1289

Freelance Visual Productions, Inc.
Box 843
Philadelphia, PA. 19105
(215) 342-1492

Freelance Photographers Guild
251 Park Avenue South
New York, NY. 10010

Gamma/Liason
150 E. 58th Street
New York, NY. 10155
(212) 888-7272

Globe Photos, Inc.
275 7th Avenue
New York, NY. 10001
(212) 689-1340

Audrey Hollyman
300 E. 40th Street
New York, NY. 10016

Hot Shots Stock Shots, Inc.
309 Lesmill Road
Toronto, ONT.
Canada M3B 2V1

The Image Bank
633 3rd Avenue
New York, NY. 10017

Image Finders Photo Agency
5501-134 Abbott Street
Vancouver, B.C.
Canada V6B 2K4

International Stock Photography, Ltd.
113 E. 31st Street
New York, NY. 10016
(212) 696-4666

Keystone Press Agency, Inc.
170 5th Avenue
New York, NY. 10010

Joan Kramer
5 North Clover Drive
Great Neck, NY. 11021
(212) 224-1758

Lambert, Harold M. Studios, Inc.
Box 27310
Philadelphia, PA. 10150
(215) 224-1400

Lightwave
1430 Massachusetts Avenue
Suite 306-114
Cambridge, MA. 02138
(617) 566-0364

Magnum
251 Park Avenue South
New York, NY. 10036

Medichrome
271 Madison Avenue
New York, NY. 10016

National News Bureau
2019 Chanceller Street
Philadelphia, PA. 19103
(215) 569-0700

Omni-Photo Communications, Inc.
521 Madison Avenue
New York, NY. 10022
(212) 751-6530

Photo Associates News Service, Inc.
Box 306, Station A
Flushing, NY. 11358
(212) 619-1700

Photo File International-Comstock
32 E. 31st Street
New York, NY. 10016
(212) 889-9700

Picture Group
5 Steeple Street
Providence, RI. 02903
(401) 273-5473

Pictures International
Box 14051
Tulsa, OK. 74159
(918) 664-1339

Religious News Service Photos
104 W. 56th Street
New York, NY. 10019
(212) 315-0870

Seaphoto LTD/Planet Earth Pictures
83-84 Longacre
London, England WC2 9NG

Shasbinka Photo
501 5th Avenue
Suite 2102
New York, NY. 10017

Stock Photo and Assignment Source Book
R.R. Bowker
1180 Avenue of the Americas
New York, NY. 10036

Strawberry Media
14/B Via Venezia
80021 Afragola (NA)
Italy

Sygma Photo News
225 W. 57th Street
New York, NY. 10019
(212) 765-1820

Third Coast Stock Source
Box 92397
Milwaukee, WI. 53202
(414) 765-9442

Teenage Corner, Inc.
70-540 Gardenia Court
Rancho Mirage, CA. 92770

Underwood and Underwood
136 E. 57TH St.
New York, NY. 10036

Valan Photos
490 Dulwich Avenue
St. Lambert
Montreal, Quebec
Canada J4P 2Z4

Viewfinders
181 St. James Street
London, Ontario
Canada N6A 1W7

Wildlife Photo Bank
1530 Westlake Avenue N.
Seattle, WA. 98109

Worldwide News Service
Box 4351
Lexington, KY. 40544
606) 858-4240

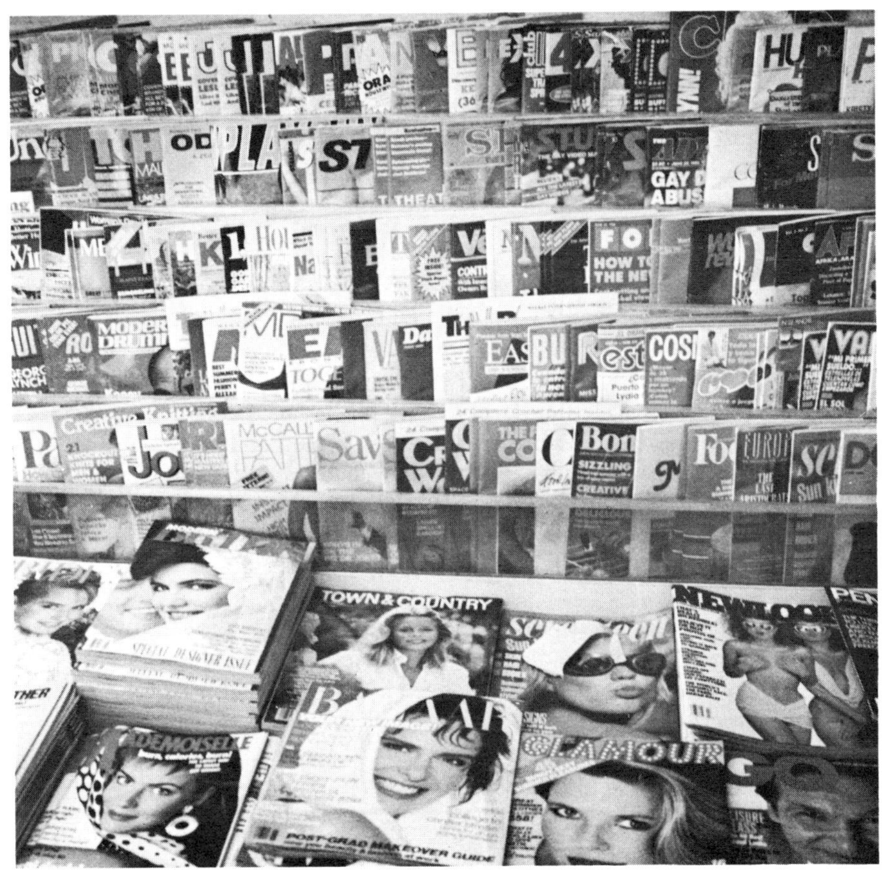

Chapter Eight—Consumer Magazines

What They Are

While any magazine that is purchased for the purpose of extracting information or simple reading enjoyment can be termed a "consumer" magazine, the term has come to mean "special interest" magazine. Magazines can be divided into two classes: general interest magazines such as *Life* and *Look*, and special interest magazines such as *Skiing* and *High Fidelity*. Most magazines are of the special interest type. Look at any newsstand display and one sees publications such as *Sailing, Popular Mechanix, Better Homes and Gardens, Modern Bride, Outdoor Life.* Note that each one concerns itself with a single interest. Most cater to the leisure-time activities of the man and woman in the street. Since the circulation varies from as little as two thousand to over 8,000,000, so do the rates for pictures vary.

How Tough Are They To Crack?

Actually, next to shooting baby pictures, these magazines constitute the best entry level for the competent freelance. Their collective requirements encompass practically any subject under the sun. Many of them, because of limited circulation and small budgets, have no objection to buying pictures that have already been published. They very seldom have use for "exclusive" rights of any kind.

In this same category (and on the other side of the coin), are magazines like *National Geographic* with a circulation of nearly 10,000,000. Their requirements are stringent and only first-class material is accepted, yet transparencies accepted for cover publication are paid for at a *minimum* of $500.00. By contrast, the publication entitled *The Arts Objectively* has an approximate circulation of 500 to a highly specialized audience. Since their circulation does not warrant the expenditure of large sums of money for photographs, their average payment per picture ranges from $2 to $5 for a 5x7 black-and-white print.

Furnishing a short written story together with his pictures will get the photographer extra dollars. So, as mentioned before, there is a level for every photographer regardless of his present skills so long as he is competent.

Should You Tackle The Big Ones?

At this writing, *Playboy* pays $600 for a full-page color photograph, and $300 for a black-and-white. So, the beginning freelance frequently falls into the trap of thinking that instead of aiming at the $10 or $25 market, he might just as well funnel his energies to producing pictures for the giants—the general interest publications such as *Playboy, TV Guide, Life,* or *National Geographic.*

The truth of the matter is that the freelance photographer has very little chance, barring unforeseen circumstances, of selling pictures to these publications. Most of their material is done on assignment, and magazine layout is done so far in advance that the likelihood of a free-lance submission fitting into their plans is highly unlikely. At the beginning, it is much more practical to aim at a target that is relatively easy to hit, and build up the experience and the contacts necessary to tackle the big markets.

Market Guide — Magazines

Magazine Directories

Ayer Directory of Publications
Ayer Press
1 Bala Avenue
Bala Cynwyd, PA. 19004

Directory of Small Magazine Press Editors and Publishers
Dustbooks
Box 1056
Paradise, CA. 95969

Magazine Industry Market Place
R.R. Bowker
1180 Avenue of the Americas
New York, NY. 10036

Photographer's Market
1933 Alliance Road
Cincinnati, OH. 45242

Photography Market Place
R.R. Bowker
1180 Avenue of the Americas
New York, NY. 10036

Standard Periodical Directory
Oxbridge Communications
183 Madison Avenue
Suite 1108
New York, NY. 10016

Consumer Magazines

Listed below you will find the names and addresses of special-interest magazines that buy freelance photography.

Adirondack Life
Box 97, Rt. 86
Jay, NY. 12941

Aim
7308 S. Eberhart Ave.
Chicago, IL. 60619

Alaska Outdoors Magazine
P.O. Box 82222
Fairbanks, AK. 99708

Alive!
Box 179
St. Louis, MO. 63166

Alternative Sources of Energy
107 S. Central Ave.
Milaca, MN. 56353

Animal Kingdom
NY Zoological Park
Bronx, NY. 10460

Archery World
225 E. Michigan
Milwaukee, WI. 53202

Architectural Digest
5900 Wilshire Blvd.
Los Angeles, CA. 90036

Atlantic Monthly
8 Arlington St.
Boston, MA.02116

Audubon Magazine
950 Third Ave.
NY., NY. 10022

Aviation Quarterly
Box 606
Plano, TX. 75074

Beauty Digest
Suite 802
126 Fifth Ave.
NY., NY. 10011

Bicycling
33 E. Minor St.
Emmaus, PA. 18049

Biology Digest
143 Old Marlton Pike
Medford, NJ. 08055

Bird Watcher's Digest
Box 110
Marietta, OH. 45750

Black America Magazine
24 Chelton Ave.
Philadelphia, PA. 19144

B'nai Brith Jewish Montthly
1640 Rhode Island Ave. NW
Washington, DC. 20036

Boating
1 Park Ave.
NY., NY. 10016

Bowhunter
3150 Mallard Cove Lane
Fort Wayne, IN. 46804

Boy's Life
Boy Scouts of America
1325 Walnut Hill Lane
Irving, TX. 75062

California Magazine
Suite 1800
11601 Wilshire Blvd.
Los Angeles, CA. 90025

Car Craft
8490 Sunset Blvd.
Los Angeles, CA. 90069

Cat Fancy
Fancy Publications, Inc.
Box 4030
San Clemente, CA. 92672

Cats Magazine
Box 37
Port Orange, FL. 32029

Child Life
Box 567
Indianapolis, IN. 46206

Christian Herald
40 Overlook Dr.
Chappaqua, NY. 10562

Coins Magazine
700 E. State St.
Iola, WI 54990

Country Magazine
Box 246
Alexandria, VA. 22313

Creative Crafts & Miniatures
Box 700
Newton, NJ. 07860

Creem
Suite 209
210 S. Woodward
Birmingham, MI 48011

Cruising World Magazine
Box 452
Newport, RI. 02840

Crusader
1548 Poplar Ave.
Memphis, TN. 38104

Deer and Deer Hunting
Box 1117
Appleton, WI. 54912

Diver Magazine
Suite 210
1807 Maritime Mews
Granville Island,
Vancouver, B.C.
Canada V6H 3W7

Dog Fancy
Box 4030
San Clemente, CA. 92672

Dolls
170 Fifth Ave.
NY., NY. 10010

Expecting Parent
685 Third Ave.
NY., NY. 10017

Family Magazine
Box 4993
Walnut Creek, CA. 94596

Farm Woman News
Box 643
Milwaukee, WI. 53201

Food & Wine
1120 Avenue of the Americas
NY., NY. 10036

Fortune
Time-Life Bldg.
NY., NY. 10020

Game & Fish Publications
Box 741
Marietta, GA. 30061

Golf Digest
5520 Park Ave. Box 0395
Trumbell, CT. 06611

Good Housekeeping
959 Eighth Ave.
NY., NY. 10019

Hadassah Magazine
50 W. 58th St.
NY., NY. 10019

Horse & Rider Magazine
41919 Moreno Rd.
Temecula, CA. 92390

Horticulture
755 Boylston St.
Boston, MA. 02116

Hot Rod Magazine
8490 Sunset Blvd.
Los Angeles, CA. 90069

House Beautiful
1700 Broadway
NY., NY. 10019

International Wildlife
1412 16th St. NW
Washington, DC. 20036

Jazziz Magazine
Box 8309
Gainesville, FL. 32605-8309

Life
Time-Life Bldg.
Rockefeller Center
NY., NY. 10020

McCall's Magazine
230 Park Ave.
NY., NY. 10169

Mother Earth News
Box 70
Hendersonville, NC. 28791

Muscle Mag International
Unit 7, 2 Melanie Dr.
Brampton, ONT.
Canada L6T 4K8

National Parks Magazine
1701 18th St. NW.
Washington DC. 20009

National Wildlife
1412 16th St. NW
Washington, DC. 20036

Natural History Magazine
Central Park West at 79th St.
NY., NY. 10024

New England Monthly
Box 446
Haydenville, MA. 01039

Nightbeat Magazine
Box 55573
Houston, TX. 77255

Ocean Realm
2333 Brickell Ave.
Miami, FL. 33129

Odyssey
Box 6227
San Jose, CA. 95150

Off-Duty America
3303 Harbor Blvd.
Suite C-2
Costa Mesa. CA. 92626

Ohio Magazine
40 S. Third St.
Columbus, OH. 43215

Oklahoma Living Magazine
Box 75579
Oklahoma City, OK. 73147

Old West
Box 2107
Stillwater, OK. 74076

Outdoor Life Magazine
380 Madison Ave.
NY., NY. 10017

Parents Magazine
685 Third Ave.
NY., NY. 10017

Pennsylvania Game News
Box 1567
Harrisburg, PA. 17105-1567

Penthouse
1965 Braodway
NY., NY. 10023-5965

Petersen's Photographic Magazine
8490 Sunset Blvd.
Los Angeles, CA. 90069

Popular Photography
1 Park Ave.
NY., NY. 10016

Popular Science
380 Madison Ave.
NY., NY. 10017

Psychic Guide
Box 701
Providence, RI. 02901

Radio-Electronics
200 Park Ave. S
NY., NY. 10003

Ranger Rick
1412 16th St. NW
Washington, DC. 20036

Rodale's New Shelter
33 E. Minor St.
Emmaus, PA. 18049

Rodeo News
Box 5418
Norman, OK. 73070

The Runner
1 Park Ave.
NY., NY. 10016

Sail
34 Commercial Wharf
Boston, MA. 02110

Saturday Review
214 Massachusetts Ave. NE.
Washington, DC. 20002

Science Digest
888 Seventh Ave.
NY., NY. 10106

Scuba
Box 6268
Pensacola, FL. 32503

Skiing Magazine
One Park Ave.
NY., NY 10016

Snowmobile Magazine
Suite 100
11812 Wayzata Blvd.
Minnetonka, MN. 55343

Soap Opera Digest
254 W. 31st. St.
NY., NY. 10001

Sport's Illustrated
Time-Life Bldg.
NY., NY. 10020

Sterling's Magazine
355 Lexington Ave.
NY., NY. 10017

Stock Car Racing Magazine
Box 715
Five Bullseye Road
Ipswich, MA. 01938

Success Magazine
342 Madison Ave.
NY., NY. 10173

Surfer Magazine
Box 1028
Dana Point, CA. 92629

Tennis Magazine
495 Westport Ave.
Norwalk, CT. 06856

Travel & Leisure
1120 Avenue of the Americas
NY., NY. 10036

Unity
Unity Village, MO. 64065

Vermont Life
61 Elm St.
Montpelier, VT. 05602

Washington Post Magazine
1150 15th St. NW.
Washington, DC. 20071

Weight Watcher's
360 Lexington Ave.
NY., NY. 10017

Western Horseman
3850 N. Nevada Ave.
Colorado Springs, CO. 80933

Western Outdoor
3197-E Airport Loop
Costa Mesa, CA. 92626

Wholistic Living News
3335 Adams Ave.
San Diego, CA. 92116

Wisconsin Sportsman
Box 2266
Oshkosh, WI. 54903

Women's Sports Magazine & Fitness
310 Town & Country Village
Palo Alto, CA. 94031

Working Mother
230 Park Ave.
NY., NY. 10169

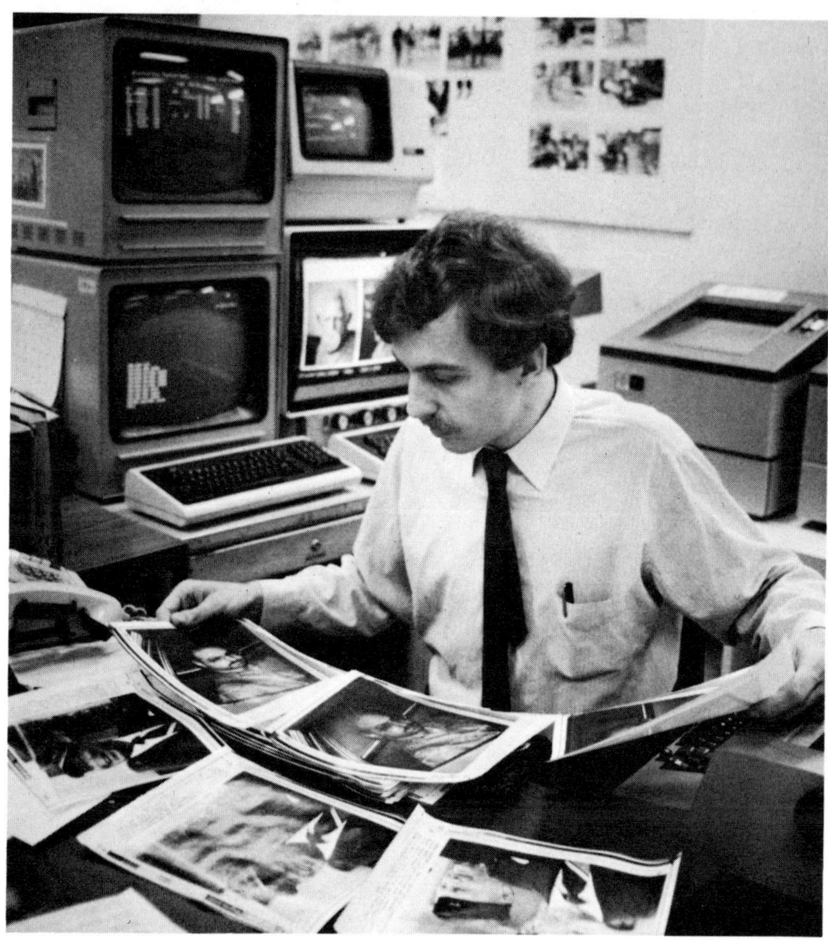

Photo Credit: Linda Cummings

Chapter Nine—Trade Journals

Sometimes Known As Business Publications

Trade journals and business publications have a specific goal. They report the latest news in a particular business or industry. They teach the distributor of a product how to increase his sales. They suggest ideas for merchandising to those retailers who handle their wares. They show the shop owner how to increase dollar volume through the use of displays and sales aids. In short, the publications deal with a particular product, service, or business.

While these magazines are wide open for the freelance photographer, it is especially important that the photographer understand the role his photographs will play in a trade journal. The pictures must be upbeat and positive. Remember, most articles in these magazines aim at flattering the image of their industry, and flat, sterile or dull shots are *out.* If a photograph of a chain hamburger outlet is portrayed, the picture should reflect a bright, clean surrounding in which the customers are obviously enjoying what is being served. A magazine dealing with antiques would certainly be prone to buying a photograph of a rare and exquisite piece provided it is attractively presented. A magazine dealing with the paint and wallpaper industry might welcome visually exciting pictures of a newly-done children's room, or a picture of a husband-and-wife team admiring the decorating job they have just completed. Magazines dealing with hair dressing are in constant need of pictures of male and female models sporting the latest hairdos.

Market Guide — Trade Journals And Business Publications

The trade journals and business publications listing which follows is merely a sampling. Complete listings (over 3000 at this writing) may be obtained at your local library by consulting a copy of BUSINESS PUBLICATION RATES AND DATA handbook. Any organization listed will supply a copy of their publication, either without charge or on payment of the cover price. Write to determine their policy.

In the advanced lessons in your NYI Course you are going to enjoy training in the *specifics* of many professional areas that are in demand by trade journals. These lessons including training in advertising photography, fashion photography, architectural and interior decorating photography, still life photography, and portrait photography of all kinds.

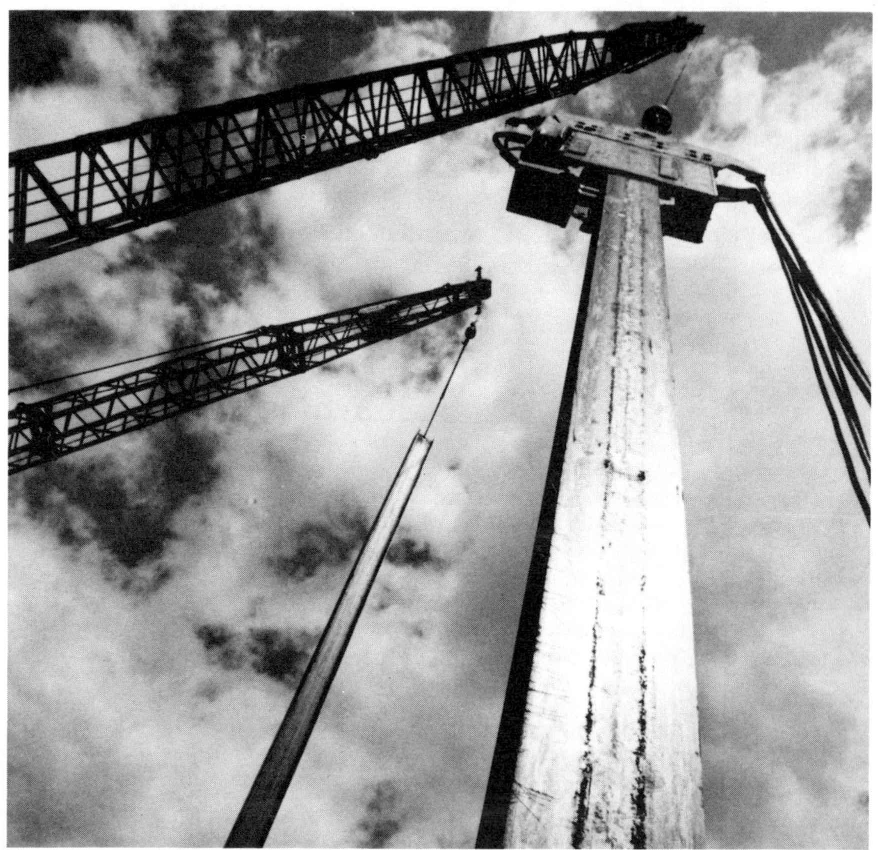

Photo Credit: Peter P. Hoeksema

Chapter Ten—House Organs

Also Known As Company Magazines

You'll never see them on a newsstand or book outlet. They are produced wholly and completely for "*in-house*" use, hence the term "*house organ.*"

While the term *house organ* has been commonly used to describe the magazine or newsletter published for internal use, the term *company magazine* is beginning to gain favor as a more contemporary and descriptive title.

What Exactly Is A Company Magazine?

A company magazine is a magazine published by any company or firm interested in promoting its particular product or service or aimed at building employee morale. It is free from outside advertising, and is distributed free to its employees, salesmen, suppliers, and stockholders.

How Does It Differ From A Trade Journal?

While a company magazine concerns itself exclusively with the product or service of one company, the trade journal encompasses a whole industry. A trade journal, for example, may concern itself with the whole field of wallpaper and decorating, while a company magazine will only deal with XYZ Paint Company and its products. Company magazines are distributed free of charge while the nature of the trade journal requires that its operating budget be obtained from the sale of advertising and from the sale of the magazine itself to people in the industry.

How Large Is The Company Magazine Field?

Very large. It is a little known fact that company magazines have a circulation that is almost three times that of *all* the newspapers in the United States *combined!* It is also little known that some of America's largest corporations may publish four, six, eight or ten *different* publications for specific areas of their operations. Stockholders receive an entirely different magazine from salesmen, and salesmen never get to see the magazine that is sent to suppliers, while an entirely different publication may go out to retailers or wholesalers.

Types of Company Publications

Company publications range from 4-page bulletin or "newsletter" to thoroughly professional slick magazines that rival *Vogue* and *Playboy* for quality of reproduction and layout.

Where To Find Your Listings

There are so many different company publications that a comprehensive list is beyond the scope of the market listings in this *Handbook.* If you are interested in this market, you can purchase a market listing covering the company magazine field exclusively. The most comprehensive and informative publication dealing with house organs or company magazines is the one published by the National Research Bureau of 424 N. Third St., Burlington, IA 52601. It is published once every three years. It lists over 4000 company publications with detailed information as to exactly what each publication is, its circulation, and specific picture requirements.

Market Guide—House Magazines

American Association of University Women
2401 Virginia Ave. NW
Washington, D.C. 20037
"Graduate Woman"

Abbott Laboratories
Abbott Park
North Chicago, IL. 60064
"Abbott Topics"

Acme Markets
124 N. 15 St.
Philadelphia, PA. 19101
"The American"

Agway, Inc.
P.O.Box 4933
Syracuse, NY. 13221
"Agway Cooperator"

Air California
3636 Birch St.
Newport Beach, CA. 92660
"Sunjet Gazette"

Alabama Gas Corp.
1918 First Ave. N
Birmingham, AL. 35203
"Gas Lines"

Allen-Bradley Co.
1201 S. Second St.
Milwaukee, WI. 53204
"Contact"

Allied Chemical
P.O. Box 2245
Morristown, NJ. 07960
"Update"

Allstate Insurance
Northbrook, IL. 60062
"Contact," "Discovery"

Aluminum Co. of America
1501 Alcoa Bldg.
Pittsburg, PA. 15219
"Alcoa News"

American Cancer Society
3316 W. 66th St.
Edina, MN. 55435
"Herald Of Hope"

American Express Co.
125 Braodway
New York, NY. 10004
"Going Places"

American Hospital Supply
One American Plaza
Evanston, IL. 60201
"Pulse"

American Iron & Steel
1000 16th St. NW
Washington, DC. 20036
"Steel"

American Motors Corp.
27777 Franklin Rd.
Southfield, MI. 48034
"AMC Update"

American Red Cross
17th and D St. NW
Washington, DC. 20006

Amtrak
400 N. Capitol St. NW
Washington, DC. 20001
"Amtrak News"

Associated Milk Producers, Inc.
Box 32287
San Antonio, TX. 78216
"Dairymen's Digest"

Atlantic Richfield Co.
515 S. Flower
Los Angeles, CA. 90071
"Arcospark"

Avis
1114 Ave. of Americas
New York, NY. 10036
"Avis News"

Bank of America
Box 37000
San Francisco, CA. 94137
"Bank American"

Baskin-Robbins
1201 S. Victory Blvd.
Burbank, CA. 91502
"Scoops"

Beech Aircraft
P.O. Box 85
Wichita, KS.
"Beechcrafter"

Blue Cross
Box 8008
Chicago, IL. 60680
"Blue Print for Health"

Braniff International
P.O. Box 61747-W125
Dallas, TX. 75261
"Bi B-Liner"

Burger King
P.O. Box 520783
Miami, FL. 33152
"Kings Page"

California Canners & Growers
3100 Ferry Bldg.
San Francisco, CA. 94106
"CCG News"

Campbell Soup Co.
375 Memorial Ave.
Camden, NJ. 08101
"Hi-Campbell"

Caterpillar Tractor Co
Peoria, IL. 61629
"Caterpillar World"

Chevrolet Motor
GMC General Motors Bldg.
Detroit, MI. 48202
"Friends"

Ciba-Geigy
444 Saw Mill River Rd.
Ardsley, NY. 10512
"On Stream"

Cooper Tire & Rubber
Lima & Western Ave.
Findlay, OH. 45840
"Tire Tracks"

Dairy Society International
3008 McKinley St. NW
Washington, DC. 20015
"DSI Bulletin"

Diners Club
10 Columbus Circle
New York, NY. 10019
"DC Currents"

Dun & Bradstreet, Inc.
299 Park Ave.
New York, NY. 10017
"Donnely Marketing News"

Eastern Airlines
Miami Airport, Bldg. 16
Miami, FL. 33148
"Falcon"

Eastman Kodak
343 State St.
Rochester, NY. 14650
"Kodakery"

Firestone Tire & Rubber
1200 Firestone Parkway
Akron, OH. 44317
"Firestone Non-Skid"

Florist Transworld
29200 NW, Box 2227
Southfield, MI. 48037
"Florist"

Ford Motor Co.
American Rd.
Dearborn, MI. 48121
"Ford World"

General Foods Corp.
250 W. St.
White Plains, NY. 10625
"GF News"

General Mills
Box 1113
Minneapolis, MN. 55440
"Family Magazine"

Georgia Ports Authority
Box 2406
Savannah, GA. 31402
"Georgia Anchorage"

Goodwill Industries
9200 Wisconsin Ave.
Bethesda, SC. 20814
"GIA News"

Gulf Oil
Gulf Bldg.
Pittsburgh, PA. 15230
"Gulf Oilmanac"

Hershey Food Corp.
14 E. Chocolate Ave.
Hershey, PA. 17033
"Avenues"

Hilton Hotels
9880 Wilshire Blvd.
Beverly Hills, CA. 90210
"Hilton Items"

Hobart Mfg.
Troy, OH. 45373
"Hobart Weldworld"

International Harvester
5565 Brookville Rd.
Indianapolis, IN. 46219
"Indy News"

International Paper Co.
220 E. 42 St.
New York, NY 10017
"Maineline"

Jarman Shoe
Genesco Park
Nashville, TN 37210
"Jarman Journal"

Kansas Dept. of Economic Development
State Office Bldg.
Topeka, KS. 66603
"Kansas!"

Lederle Laboratories
Middletown Rd.
Pearl River, NY. 10965
"Update"

Lone Star Steel Co.
E. B. Germany Works
Lone Star, TX. 75668
"Starlight"

Maine Potato Council
Box 632
Presque Island, ME. 04769
"Potato Councillor"

Manufacturing Chemists Assn.
1825 Conn Ave. NW
Washington, DC. 20009
"Chemecology"

Miller Brewing Co.
3939 Highland Blvd.
Milwaukee, WI. 53208
"Miller Time"

Mack Trucks, Inc.
Box M
Allentown, PA. 18105
"Mack Bulldog"

Mobil Oil
150 E. 42 St.
NY., NY. 10017
"Mobil World Compass"

Oscar Mayer & Co.
Madison, WI. 53707
"Link"

Owens-Corning Fiberglass
Fiberglass Tower
Toledo, OH. 43659
"Dialog"

Pan American World Airways
Pan Am Bldg.
200 Park Ave.
NY., NY. 10166
"Clipper"

Pepsi-Cola
Anderson Hill Rd.
Purchase, NY. 10577
"Pepsi-Cola World"

Phillip Morris, Inc.
120 Park Ave.
New York, NY. 10017
"Call News"

Pillsbury Co.
MS 3266 Pillsbury Center
Minneapolis, MN. 55402
"Pillsbury Reporter"

Pfizer
235 E. 42 St.
New York, NY.
"Pfizer Scene"

Quaker Oats Co.
345 Merchandise Mart Plaza
Chicago, IL. 60654
"Grocery"

Radio Shack
1300 One Tandy Center
Fort Worth, TX. 76102
"Intercom"

Ralston Purina
Checkerboard Square
St. Louis, MO. 63188
"Ralston Purina Magazine"

RCA Corporation
30 Rockefeller Center
New York, NY. 10020
"Communicate"

Reynolds Metal
Reynolds Metals Bldg.
Richmond, VA. 23261
"Reynolds Review"

Roadway Express Co.
1077 Gorge Blvd.
Akron, OH. 44309
"Spotlight"

Safeway Stores
201 4th St.
Oakland, CA. 94660
"Safeway News"

Salvation Army
503 E. St. NW
Washington, DC. 20001
"On The Scene"

Santa Fe Railroad
80 E. Jackson Blvd.
Chicago, IL. 60604
"Santa Fe Magazine"

Schwinn Bicycle Co.
1856 N. Kostner Ave.
Chicago, IL. 60639
"Schwinn Reporter"

Scott Paper Co.
Scott Plaza
Philadelphia, PA. 19113
"Scott Impact"

Swank Jewelry
Attleboro, MA. 02703
"Link"

Texas Instruments
Dallas, TX. 75265
"Ti-Dallasite"

Todd Shipyards
1801 16th SW
Seattle, WA. 98124
"Todd News"

Tupperware
Box 751 Drawer D
Woonsocket, RI. 02895
"Tupperware Topics"

United States Army
Cameron Station Bldg.
Alexandria, VA. 22314
"Soldiers"

Virginia Poultry Federation
Box 1036
Harrisonburg, VA. 22801
"Virginia Poultryman"

VW pf America
888 W. Big Beaver
Troy, MI. 48084
"VW Mirror"

Warner-Lambert Pharmaceutical Co.
201 Tabor Rd.
Morris Plains, NJ. 07950
"Warner-Lambert World"

Zenith Radio Corp.
1900 N. Austin Ave.
Chicago, IL. 60639

Directories

Business Publication Rates and Data
Standard Rate and Data Service
5201 Old Orchard Road
Skokie, IL. 60077

Consumer Magazine and Farm Publication Rates and Data
Standard Rate and Data Service
5201 Old Orchard Road
Skokie, IL. 60077

Harfax Directory of Industry Data Sources
Ballinger Publishing Co.
Box 281, 54 Church Street
Cambridge, MA. 02138

O'Dwyer's Directory of Corporate Communications
1 R. O'Dwyer Co.
271 Madison Avenue
New York, NY. 10016

Photo Market Reference

Photographer's Market
Writer's Digest Books
9933 Alliance Rd.
Cincinnati, OH. 45242

Photography Market Place
R.R. Bowker
1180 Avenue of the Americas
New York, NY. 10036

General Trade Journals

American Cinematographer
P.O. Box 2230
Hollywood, CA. 90078

Animal Health & Nutrition
Sandstone Bldg.
Mount Morris, IL. 61054

Antiques Dealer
1115 Clifton Ave.
Clifton, NJ. 07013

Aviation Week & Space Technology
1221 Ave. of the Americas
New York, NY. 10020

Beauty Fashion
48 E. 43 St.
New York, NY. 10017

Brake & Front End
11 S. Forge St.
Akron, OH. 44303

California Veterinarian
655 University Ave. #115
Sacramento, CA. 90078

Collision
Box 389
Framingham, MA. 02038

Dairy Foods
President's Plaza
8750 W. Bryn Mawr Ave.
Chicago, IL. 60631

Dixie Contractor
525 Marshall Ave.
Decatur, GA. 30031

Electronic Engineering Times
600 Community Dr.
Manhasset, NY. 11030

Farm & Power Equipment
9701 Gravois Ave.
St. Louis, MO. 63123

Fire Chiefs Magazine
40 E. Huron St.
Chicago, IL. 60611

Golf Industry
1545 NE 123rd St.
North Miami, FL. 33161

Industry Week
1111 Chester Ave.
Cleveland, OH 44114

Instructor Magazine
545 Fifth Ave.
New York, NY. 10017

Journal Of Family Practice
25 Van Zant St.
East Norwalk, CT. 06855

Journal of Reading
800 Barksdale Road
Newark, DE. 19714

Law & Order
100 Skokie Blvd.
Wilmette, Il 60091

Learning
1111 Bethlehem Pike
Springhouse, PA. 19477

Model Retailer
Clifton House
Clifton, VA. 22024

Owner Operator Magazine
Chilton Co.
Radnor, PA. 19089

Photomethods
50 S. 9th St.
Minneapolis, MN. 55402

Professional Photographer
1090 Executive Way
Des Plaines, IL. 60018

Quick Frozen Foods
271 Madison Ave.
New York, NY. 10016

Science and Children
1742 Connecticut Ave NW.
Washington, D.C. 20009

Wallcoverings Magazine
15 Bank St.
Stamford, CT. 06901

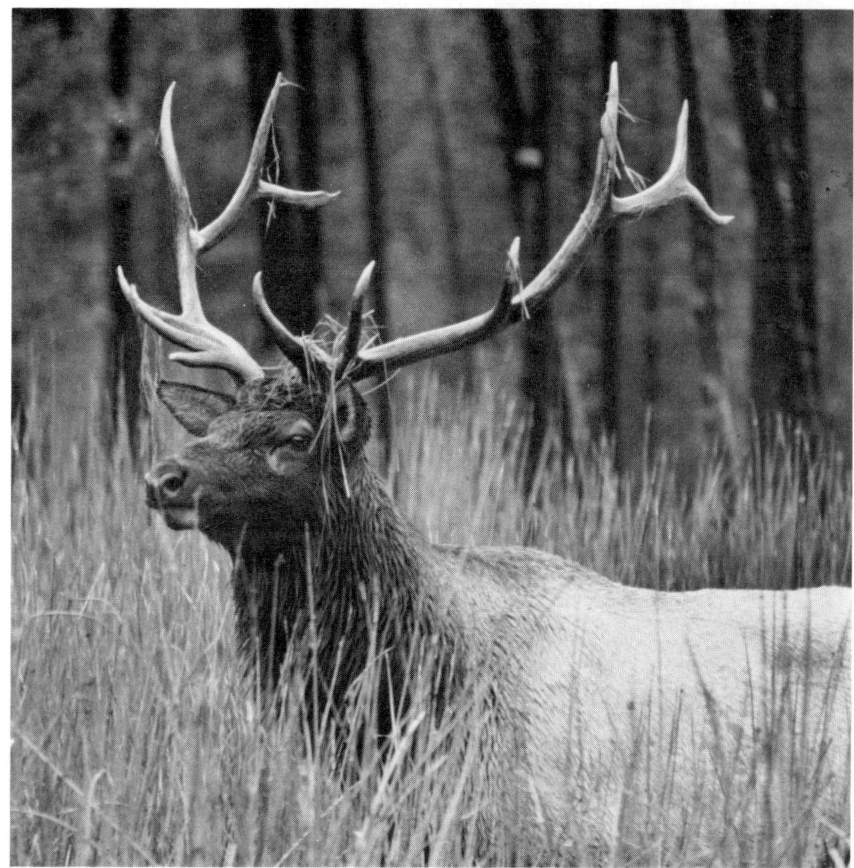

Photo Credit: Mike Brooks

Chapter Eleven— The Calendar Market

Choose Your Photographs Carefully

One of the most lucrative markets for color transparencies is the calendar market. Thousands of color slides of pretty girls, children, and scenics are used each year to supply calendar manufacturers with the variety they need to keep their sales volume high. Transparencies for calendar sales must be sharp and full of bold color. They must be able to get the viewer's attention and *hold* it. Pictures designed for calendar use must have the same qualities as those for posters and magazine covers—*impact!*

Study Your Market

While general subjects adequately meet the needs of a majority of calendar manufacturers, more and more are beginning to specialize in the custom calendar—that calendar which is tailored to the product or services of a particular business. Many banks, food manufacturers and insurance companies select the *theme* they would like for their calendars. This may include wild animals, flowers of the forest, food favorites of many lands, or different species of butterflies. It is very important to know what the buyer wants.

Shoot For Tomorrow

Of all picture users, the calendar manufacturer has the longest ''lead time'' of practically anyone else. The picture he intends using next year or the year after is bought *today.* It makes sense then that your subject matter should be the type that can stand the test of time. Good landscapes, animals, and children are perennial favorites.

When Not To Submit

Since the months of November, December, January and February are normally given over to production of calendars and subsequent ''mop-up'' activities, most manufacturers prefer that submissions be made after the end of February and throughout the year until the end of October. Don't submit winter pictures in October, November, and December—it's too late. Pictures depicting snow scenes should be mailed in June or July and photographs of people at the beach should be submitted in October or March or sooner.

Related Markets

If you are successful in producing photographs for the calendar market, then it is good business to take a good look at other ''paper product'' markets such as greeting cards, jigsaw puzzles, playing cards, posters, wallpaper designs, stationary and postcards. The market requirements are very similar so that a photograph that is turned down by a manufacturer of one product may be purchased by another.

Market Guide — Calendars

Golden Turtle Press
1619 Shattuck Ave.
Berkley, CA. 94709

Grand Rapids Calendar Company
906 S. Division Avenue
Grand Rapids, MI. 49507

Midwest Art Publishers
1123 Washington Ave.
St. Louis, MI. 63101

Mike Roberts Color Productions
2033 8th Street
Berkeley, CA. 94710

Sierra Club Books
730 Polk Street
San Francisco, CA. 94109

Sormani Calendars
613 Waverly Ave.
Mamaroneck, NY. 10543

Wisconsin Tales and Trails
Box 5650
Madison, WI.53705

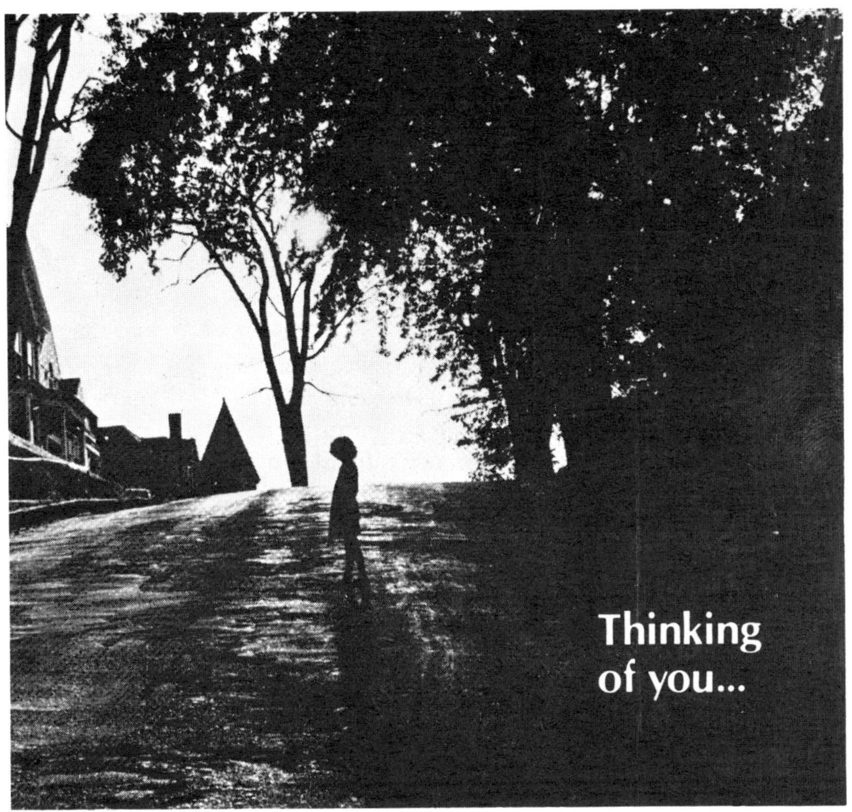

Chapter Twelve—
Paper Product Market

Greeting Cards

While many photographs made for calendar use are similar in approach and content to those used for greeting cards, the card market changes more dramatically and more often. The greeting card market has its fingers on the pulse of the contemporary scene: ecology; boy meets girl; love and romance each take their regular turns in being featured on the face of the greeting card. While a standard base is maintained, using the solid favorites such as children and scenics, a large portion of greeting card production is aimed at an elusive and ever-changing marketplace. Take the time to seek out and study card displays. Note how often misty young love is portrayed in a variety of fashions and approaches. "I love you" . . . "I miss you" . . . "Waiting for your return" are all captions that leap out at you from every other card. The subject matter may be a couple strolling on the beach, or a gull flying into the sun, or a young girl looking out a rain-spattered window. Soft-focus has been the vogue for the last few years, and this technique will probably stay popular until it wears itself out and is replaced by something more in line with changed public fancy.

Don't Forget The Standards!

While searching for misty young love, don't forget those photographs that are in vogue year in and year out—the flowers of the season, sunset, sunrise, and peaceful and seductive scenics, warm puppies, and cuddly kittens.

More Paper Products Markets

The paper market includes jigsaw puzzles, wrapping paper designs, box designs, playing cards, and place mats. The last few years have seen an upsurge in picture buying by manufacturers of plastic cubes designed to hold six photographs. While rates are not high, it is a relatively easy market in which to get beginning experience. Visit a store that has a plastic-cube display and look at the name of the manufacturer, which is usually imprinted somewhere on the product. Drop a line and ask for permission to submit some of your samples.

Posters

In recent years, the poster market has grown fantastically. Many of the top sellers are pictures of celebrities—rock stars, movie and TV personalities, and sports figures. These are probably not a potential market for you. But many others portray subjects of general interest—animals, scenics, babies, humor, and so forth. Again, explore the market. See what's being offered for sale. Ask storekeepers which pictures are their hottest sellers. Check the names of the manufacturers in the copyright notice on the poster. And, if you think you've got the type of pictures a given manufacturer may want, write him!

Paper Products Directories

Decor Sources Annual
Commerce Publishing Co.
408 Olive Avenue
St. Louis, MO. 63102

Gift & Decorative Accessory Buyer's Guide Directory
Geyer McAllister Publications
51 Madison Ave.
New York, NY. 10036

Interior Design Buyer's Guide
Interior Design Publications
805 Third Avenue
New York, NY. 10022

Paper Product Buyers—Murals, Packaging Design, Decorative Objects.

Abbey Press
St. Meinrad, IN. 57577
Greeting cards, stationery

Africa Card Company
303 W. 42nd Street
New York, NY. 10036
Greeting Cards

American Giftline Corp.
Box 472
Brockton, MA. 02402
Greeting cards, stationery

Ben-Mont Corporation
Ben-Mont Avenue
Bennington, VT. 05201
Specialty giftwrap

Golden Rod Press
704 Pine Avenue
Kemmerer, WY. 83101
Stationery

Papercraft Corporation
Papercraft Park
Pittsburgh, PA. 15238
Giftwrap, Christmas cards

Warner Press, Inc.
1200 E. 5th Street
Anderson, IN. 46012
Church bulletins

Posters

Argus Communications
7440 Natachez Avenue
Niles, IL. 60648

Arthur A. Kaplan, Co.
460 W. 34th St.
New York, NY. 10001

Bernard Picture Co.
Box 4744
Largo Park
Stanford, CT. 06907

International Graphics
2901 Simms Street
Hollywood, FL. 33022

Landmark General Corp.
Suite 227, Box 1100
Sausalito, CA. 94966

Rockshots
632 Broadway
New York, NY. 10012

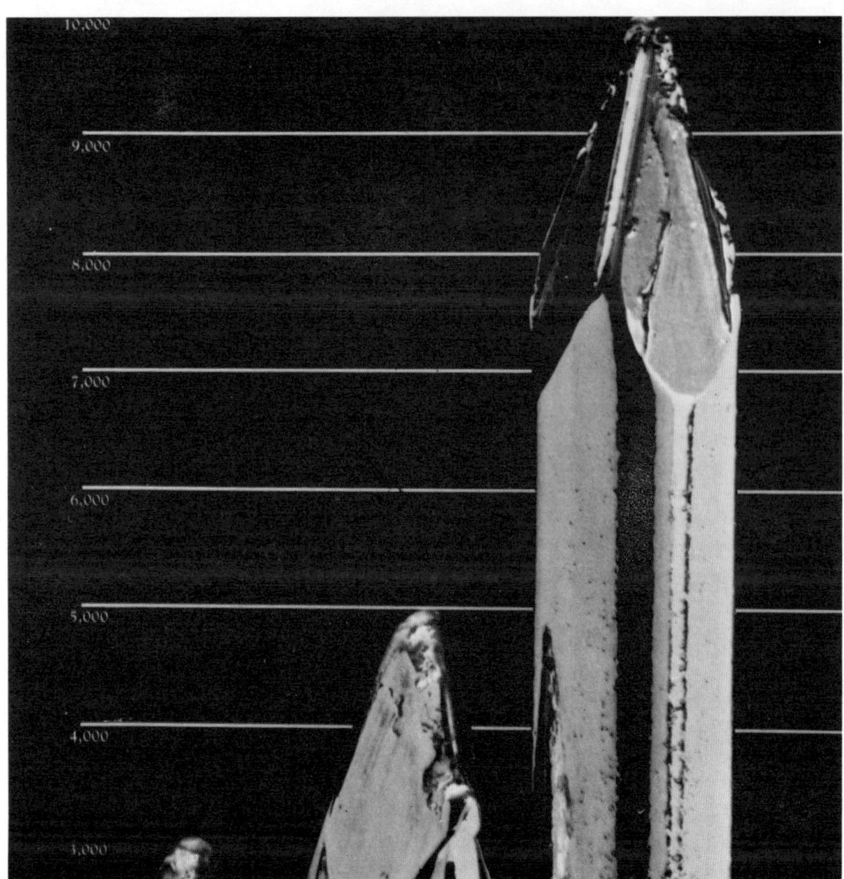

Chapter Thirteen—The Annual Report

How Times Have Changed

There was a time long ago when large companies issued reports to their stockholders consisting of row upon row of figures and statistics. Investors were assumed to base their investment portfolios on what these figures contained. Lo and behold, some bright guy discovered that in order to interest people in a particular company it might be a good idea to *sell* him the company. Thus, today's slick version of the annual report was born. Annual reports became thicker and more informative. While, by SEC regulation, the figures still had to be in the report, photographs began to also find their way into the pages. Editors began to tell stockholders and their friends about the company and its employees—its present state and its future goals—all in easy-to-see and tempting picture layouts. The emphasis has changed from numbers to people!

More Specifically

An annual report issued by a steel corporation might still contain *formal portraits* of the company's corporate officers. It would, however, also contain something more important. It would show some of those corporate officers talking to the foreman in the shop while a ton of molten steel is pouring through the forming rollers. It might show an executive and an engineer looking over a set of blueprints at the site of an expansion project. It might show another executive giving out a silver cup to the winner of the potato sack race at the company's annual picnic. The idea? Sell an image of corporate and employee cooperation and solidity—of well-being—of a family rather than just employer and employee. It's the kind of image that makes an investor want to cast his lot with the company. He rightfully concludes that a happy group makes a good product!

The annual report also shows the company's products in use, depicting happy satisfied customers. It shows the results of the company's charitable activities—the ballet troupe it subsidizes, the hospital, the medical research. In other words, it shows people benefitting from being touched by the company. The annual report has become a tool for attracting new investors by depicting the company as an active contributing part of the community, the nation, the world.

What Is The Most Effective Format Used?

What method does the annual report use to tell this story of service? The same method and format used by the photojournalist when he produces an essay. The story is told in *pictures!* It is told in the most effective visual sequence, using imaginative techniques and solid technical disciplines. There is room to be both factual and creative. The techniques of double exposure, multiple flash, soft focus, and good composition are all tools at the disposal of the photographer who is lucky enough to draw an annual report as an assignment.

How About Quality?

As with many company publications, budgets vary considerably. Some annual reports still contain a formal portrait of a corporate officer, plus the facts and figures previously mentioned as being required by law. On the other side of the scale are those major corporations with unlimited amounts of money to spend who do not hesitate at spending $1000 a day or more to hire the best talent available. Their publications are slick and glossy—filled with exquisite color photographs that rival in quality and layout the most prestigious consumer magazines. Top-flight art directors lend their talents to produce evocative layouts that can only be described as mouth-watering. Needless to state, in such publications only the best photography can survive. The beginning freelance is advised to do his basic training with low-budget publications where the requirements are not as stringent as in the top-drawer annual report publications. Remember that the annual report is, when all is said and done, a public relations and advertising publication in which "best foot forward" is the catchword and where there are many watchdogs whose job it is to see that the company's best foot *is* forward.

Directory

O'Dwyer's Directory of Corporate Communications
1 R. O'Dwyer Co.
271 Madison Ave.
New York, NY. 10016

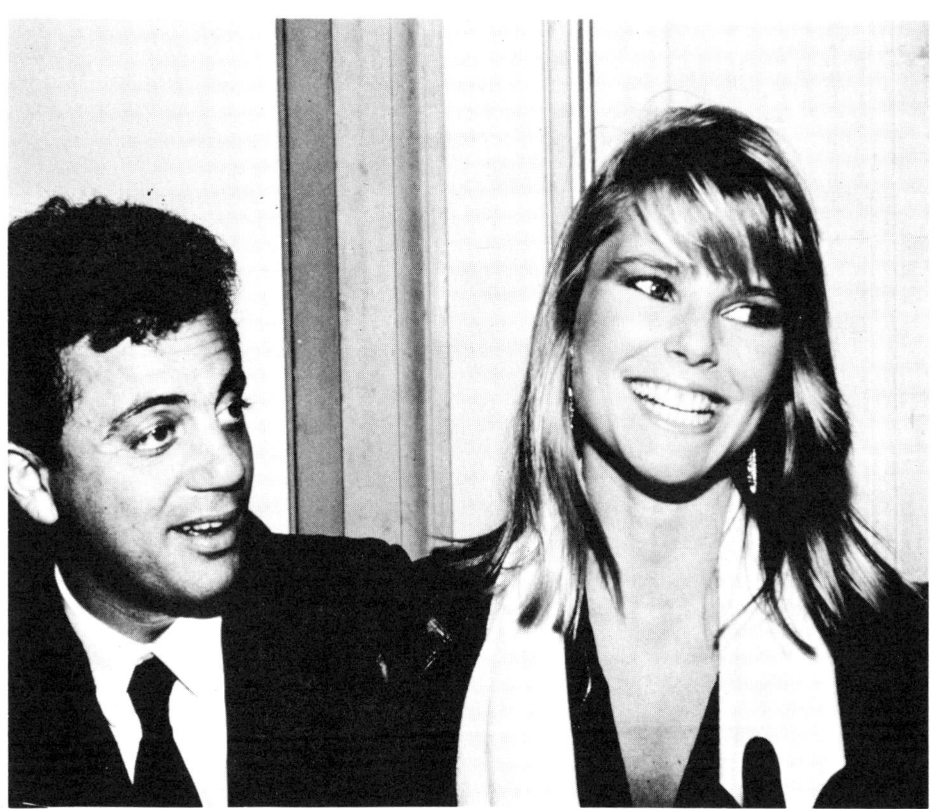

Chapter Fourteen— Public Relations

A Definition

While the annual report is a major public relations effort where the finished product is bound and distributed, there are many other types of public relations photographs. The brochure you read showing a boy and girl on a lake is *public relations* for the bungalow colony which fronts the lake. They want you to visit *their* bungalow colony and become the boy and girl in the canoe. High school seniors are deluged with mailing pieces from almost every college in the country showing their campuses and study rooms, their cafeterias and libraries, their athletic fields and tree-shaded walks. They are public relations photographs—designed to induce the senior to enroll. A public relations assignment might consist of a single photograph showing the mayor and the head of an architectural firm joining in a symbolic digging of the first shovel of earth at the site of a proposed hospital or school.

Public relations photographs are really first cousins to news pictures and are often published in daily newspapers in addition to the company-sponsored publication or newsletter. The expression *business photography* is often heard as a substitute for *public relations*, but they are substantially the same kind of photography. I doubt that any person in the United States has not seen the picture of one guy handing a plaque to another for some service or deed rendered—this is public relations.

The Public Relations Man

The old image of the PR man was that of a cigar-chewing dynamo. Today, he's more likely a college graduate in a three-piece suit. But his objective is the same as before: To get as many pictures of the product or service or organization before the public eye as is humanly possible. They get paid to attract the public's gaze and to *keep* it. Since they dispense pictures without charge to as many sources as they possibly can, they are in constant need of fresh photographs. While this is not usually a high-paying market, it *is* one in which the freelance can acquire experience, training, and make valuable contacts.

There Are Some Drawbacks

Since the PR man gives photographs to almost anyone who asks (and gives them without charge), it is not unlikely that a photographer will see a picture he sold for $10 reproduced in a newspaper or magazine. He will wonder if he was cheated in some manner. The truth is probably "No." While some loss of control of the photographer's pictures may take place in the public relations market, the photographer may arm himself with some protections. He may insist that while the public relations firm or individual use the photograph as they wish editorially, that they may *not* use it for advertising *and* that rights for future use always remain with him (the photographer). This makes it possible for the photographer to use the picture for his own purposes some time in the future if he so desires. In other words, he does *not* surrender ownership of the photograph. This is a valuable right to retain. A fuller discussion of rights, what they are, and how to handle them, appears in a subsequent chapter.

A Training Area For The Beginner

In almost every town, big or small, there are various clubs and organizations that run annual fund-raising drives. They distribute brochures and leaflets as part of their campaigns to alert the general public to their aims and goals. Often a single picture will be incorporated into a brochure describing in detail what the particular organization is promoting. Volunteer fire departments and women's auxiliaries, 4-H clubs and church groups, Little League and Girl Scouts all cry for photographs. Since their budgets are limited and sometimes non-existent, the enterprising freelance may offer to furnish a free photograph, taking as compensation the publicity that will accrue to him. He should insist that his byline be printed below the photograph. At the beginning of a career, exposure to as many people as possible is almost as important as immediate compensation in the form of money. As people get to know you as a competent photographer, casual acquaintances may blossom into paying clients.

Market Guide—Public Relations

Your first source is likely to be the local Yellow Pages or the Yellow Pages of the largest community nearby. Additionally, you may want to consult the following sources, available at the Public Library:

Contact Book for the Entertainment Industry
Celebrity Service, Inc.
171 W. 57th St.
New York, NY. 10019

International Buyer's Guide of the Music-Tape Industry
Billboard Productions
1515 Broadway
New York, NY. 10036

New York Publicity Outlets
Public Relations Plus, Inc.
Box 327
Washington Depot, CT. 06794

Photographer's Market
9933 Alliance Rd.
Cincinnati, OH. 45242

Register of the Public Relations Societies of America
845 Third Ave.
New York, NY. 10022

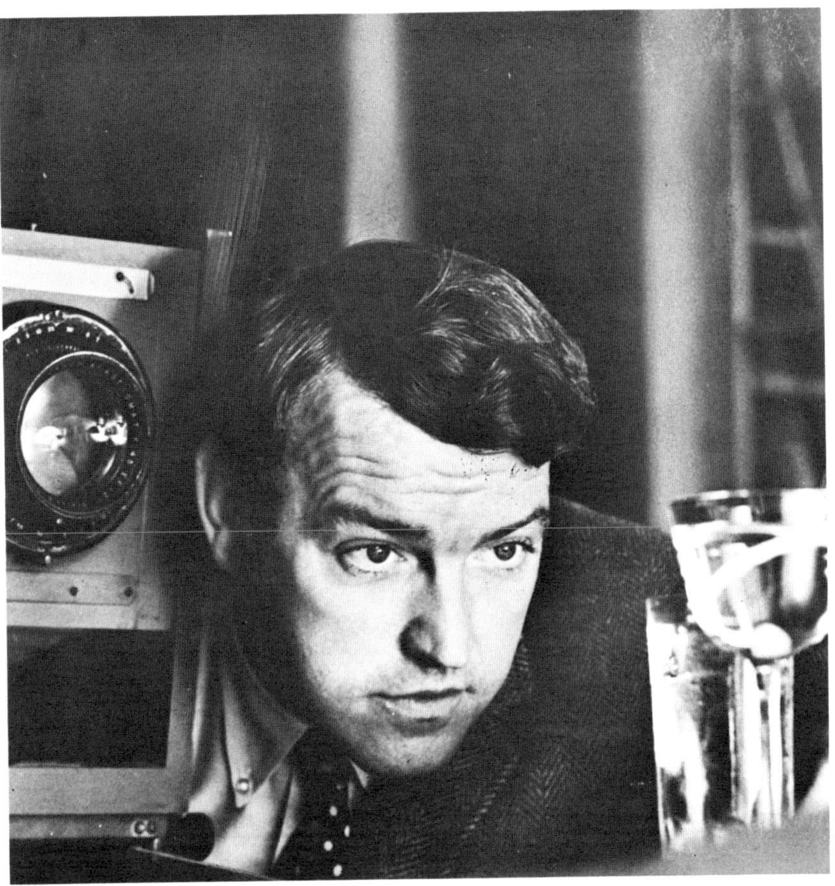

Chapter Fifteen— The Advertising Market

It's Not Easy

There has never been born the photographer in whose breast has not been nurtured the dream of commanding high fees, directing exquisite models, and traveling to far-off places. Of all the avenues of success open to the freelance photographer, there is none which is as demanding of top-notch skills and disciplines as the advertising field. Advertising photographers, almost without exception, need a studio, elaborate equipment, and extensive support personnel to compete successfully in the marketplace. Even the production of what may seem to be a routine photograph requires unbelievable execution of a myriad of details. A picture of two men talking in the street may require days to secure the right models, wait for the correct lighting conditions and the correct flow of traffic (according to the original concept of the art director). Clothing is carefully chosen as is the exact spot where the conversation is to take place. A styling coordinator may wait outside camera range, ready to dart in and adjust a tie or sweep back a wisp of stray hair. An advertising photographer may be asked to execute near-impossible winter scenes in the middle of summer or create a sweltering beach scene in near-zero weather. Photographing a cold drink may mean having on hand hundreds of ice cubes to replace the ones that are melting while the photographer is positioning his lights, or "creating" ice cubes from acrylic.

It Also Requires Money

While the world of the advertising photographer is one in which large fees are dispensed in a routine manner, it is also one with a high mortality rate. Individuals or partnerships too often derive large parts of their income from one or two clients. Should they lose an account, they are forced to scurry for new business to avoid disaster. Initial investments are high and upkeep a necessary evil. It is a world in which only the truly hardy survive the constant worry and aggravation which is part of the advertising photographer's existence. Dealing with models and art directors is far from a bed of roses. From time to time, the freelance who has achieved expertise in the photojournalistic area may get an assignment where naturalness and simplicity are the keynotes of an ad campaign. In these instances, he may find himself earning higher fees for doing essentially the same kind of photographs he might have done for an essay. But these opportunities are rare for the unknown freelance.

Creativity Is Important

Yet opportunity does exist, especially with smaller advertisers. If you get such an assignment, use it as an opportunity to express your totality of technical and creative talent. While almost all assignments received by an advertising photographer are full of detailed instructions as to what the client wants, it is the photographer with flair who becomes successful. Within the framework of the clients needs is ample room for the "personal touch." The quality that separates the ordinary photographer from the successful illustrator is the ability to impart a special "something" to a seemingly routine job. (Most ads are routine, you know.) It may be that one photographer has the knack of extracting expressions from models that nobody else can. Some commercial photographers discover that they are good with kids. Others have the knack of extending or elaborating on the client's instructions without wandering outside the borders of what is required, and thus are able to furnish an infinite number of variations on the same theme. Still another photographer may be blessed with a gift for direction and be able to communicate the needs of his client to the models he works with so that they understand quickly and clearly what is required—a priceless asset that saves time and money and results in photographs that are story-telling and natural.

There Are Many Levels

As in every other photographic area, advertising budgets, requirements and procedures vary from company to company and from agency to agency. The giant corporations with unlimited funds to expend on national ad campaigns begin by hiring photographers with known reputations and a history of successes. They will form a "team" consisting of photographer, stylist, art director, a variety of assistants and make-up people. The campaign is laid out as carefully and as painstakingly as a major battle, with each person on the team assigned the responsibility of doing a particular task.

On the other side of the coin are those smaller companies whose requirements may be limited to a dozen pictures a year to be placed in local newspapers. Remuneration for the photographer is considerably lower in these areas, but the chances of getting frequent assignments are increased. Small firms usually dispense with the services of everyone except that person who is required to produce the picture they need—the photographer. It is not at all uncommon for small accounts to work directly with the freelance, bypassing the advertising agency. Since the amount of money they have to spend is minimal, they take the shortest route from concept to finished product. While enormous sums are expended annually in the advertising field, it is usually not recommended that the beginning freelance make this his primary target. Discover your strengths and weaknesses and explore your preferences and goals. If advertising photography is really where you want to go, examine yourself to determine if you possess the technical and artistic skills, the disciplines, and the patience required to make the grade. It's tough!

You receive a complete lesson in *Advertising Photography* in your NYI Course. What's more, you are also trained in how to use a view camera—a skill that may become essential if you are really serious about making a career in the advertising industry.

Market Guide—Advertising

Magazines and Directories

Adweek
230 Park Avenue
New York, NY. 10022

Advertising Age
740 Rush Street
Chicago, IL. 60611

Advertising Art Buyers of America
G.P.O. Box 1491
New York, NY. 10001

American Showcase, Inc.
724 Fifth Avenue
New York, NY. 10019
(212) 245-0981

American Society of Picture Professionals Directory
Box 5283, Grand Central Station
New York, NY. 10017

Art Directors Annual
Art Directors Club
22 East 31st Street
New York, NY. 10016

Art Director's Index To Photography
John S. Butsch Assoc.
415 West Superior Street
Chicago, IL. 60610

Advertising Yellow Pages
"The Bluebooks"
New York Yellow Pages, Inc.
113 University Place
New York, NY. 10003

Audoivisual Market Place
R.R. Bowker
1180 Avenue of the Americas
New York, NY. 10036

The Book (New England)
PO Box 749
431 Post Road East
Westport, CT. 06880

Creative Blackbook, Inc.
401 Park Avenue South
New York, NY. 10016
(212) 684-4255

Creative Directory (Mid-West)
333 North Michigan Avenue
Suite 311
Chicago, IL. 60603

The Creative Directory of the Sun Belt
Ampersad Incorporated
1103 South Shepard Drive
Houston, TX. 77019

Madison Avenue Handbook
17 East 48th Street
New York, NY. 10017

Workbook
940 North Highland Avenue
Los Angeles, CA. 90038
(213) 856-0008

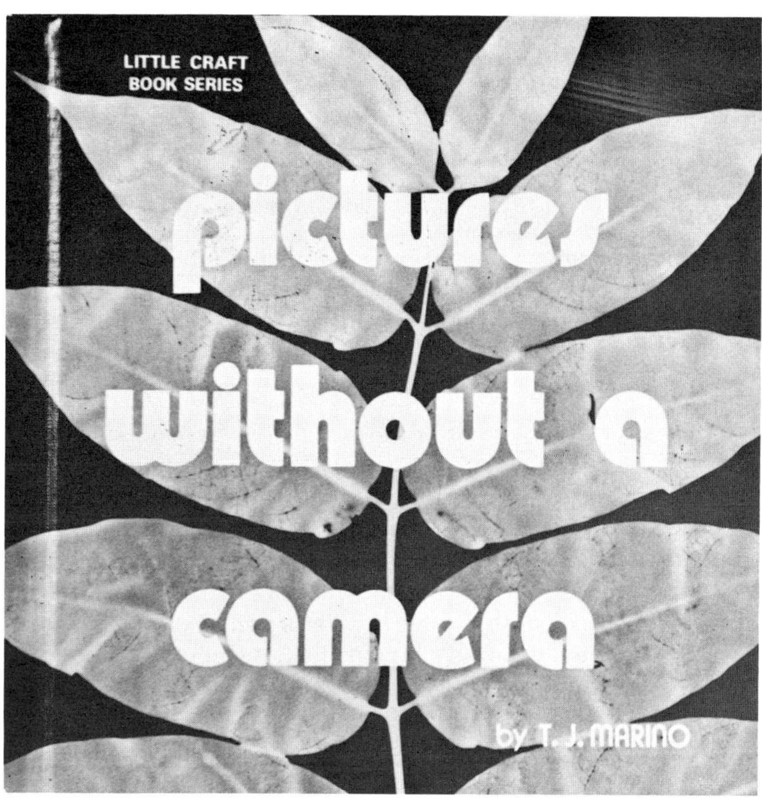

Chapter Sixteen—
Publishing Your Own Book

Start With An Idea

For some photographers, the single picture or the occasional assignment is not enough. They require something they can sink their teeth into over an extended period of time. These photographers thrive on producing a photographic essay in book form.

Is there something you really like? Racing cars? Old locomotives? Parades? The possible extinction of a wilderness animal? Our disappearing forests? How kids relate to each other? Unmarried couples?

Why not create your own book?

Photographer Herb Goro took a single city block in the Bronx and produced a well-received book on the daily lives of its inhabitants. Bruce Davidson produced a similar book entitled East 110th Street, and New York-based Photographer Diane Arbus (now deceased) was immortalized by a monograph of her favorite pictures.

How About A Collaborator?

It is indeed a rare photographer who is also a good writer, and many themes demand the inclusion of printed words to emerge as a whole salable package. A sensitive writer well may be what you need for the perfect "other half" of your team. If you think alike and feel the same way about certain things, the marriage might produce a body of work, which when combined, is more powerful than the sum of its parts.

Poetry and pictures have been natural companions since the first printing press was invented. A poet with a soul and a photographer with imagination can combine successfully to produce a salable book.

How About Publishing?

While the actual printing and distribution of a book are outside the capabilities of the average team, a "dummy" book is not. Pasting up words and text to form a rough sample is the best way to present this kind of work. Place pictures (in actual size) exactly where they work to best advantage and surround them with text and captions in just the manner in which they would appear when they come off the printing press. Go to a photographic book store and examine all the books for *layout.* When you find a layout that appeals to you and that will be appropriate for your subject, use it as your model.

Your pasted-up dummy is now your sample or presentation piece. Make the rounds of all the publishers you can find. If your book is well done, *someone* will want to publish it. Publishers also possess the means for distribution, without which the book cannot reach a desired audience.

A project of this sort is a major undertaking, and solid basic training and accomplished skills should precede any attempt to enter this field.

Market Guide — Book Publishers

Educational Directories

American Universities and Colleges
American Council on Education
1 Dupont Circle
Washington, DC. 20036

Association for Educational Communication and Technology Directory
1126 16th Street N.W.
Washington, DC. 20036

Educational Marketter Yellow Pages
Knowledge Industry Publications
2 Corporate Park Drive
White Plains, NY. 10604

Book Publishers

Addison House
Morgan's Run
Danbury, NH. 03230

Amphoto
1515 Broadway
New York, NY. 10036

Aperture Monographs
20 E. 23 St.
New York, NY. 10022

Craftsman Book Co.
6058 Corte Del Cedro
Carlsbad, CA. 92008

Delmar Publishers
2 Computer Dr. W.
Albany, NY. 12212

Focal Press
80 Montvale
Stoneham, MA. 02180

David Godine
306 Dartmouth St.
Boston, MA. 02116

Golden West Books
Box 80250
San Marino, CA. 91108

H.P. Books
Box 5367
Tucson, AZ. 85703

Light Impressions
Box 3012
Rochester, NY. 14614

Morgan & Morgan
145 Palisade St.
Dobbs Ferry, NY. 10522

New York Graphic Society
11 Beacon St.
Boston, MA. 02108

101 Productions
834 Mission St.
San Francisco, CA. 94103

Ortho Books
575 Market St.
San Francisco, CA. 94105

Outdoor Empire Publishing
Box C-19000
Seattle, WA. 98109

Padre Productions
Box 1257
San Luis Obispo, CA. 93406

Pelican Publishing
1101 Monroe St.
Gretna, LA. 70053

Zondervan Publishing
1415 Lake Drive
Grand Rapids, MI. 49506

Directories of Book Publishers

American Book Trade Directory
R.R. Bowker
1180 Avenue of the Americas
New York, NY. 10036

The Bowker Annual of Library and Book Publishers
R.R. Bowker
1180 Avenue of the Americas
New York, NY. 10036

Directory of Small Magazine Press Editors and Publishers
Dustbooks
Box 1056
Paradise, CA. 95969

Directory of West Coast Book Publishers
Creative Options
Box 601
Edmonds, WA. 98020

Literary Market Place
R.R. Bowker
1180 Avenue of the Americas
New York, NY. 10036

Writers Market
Writers Digest Books
9933 Alliance Rd.
Cincinnati, OH. 45242

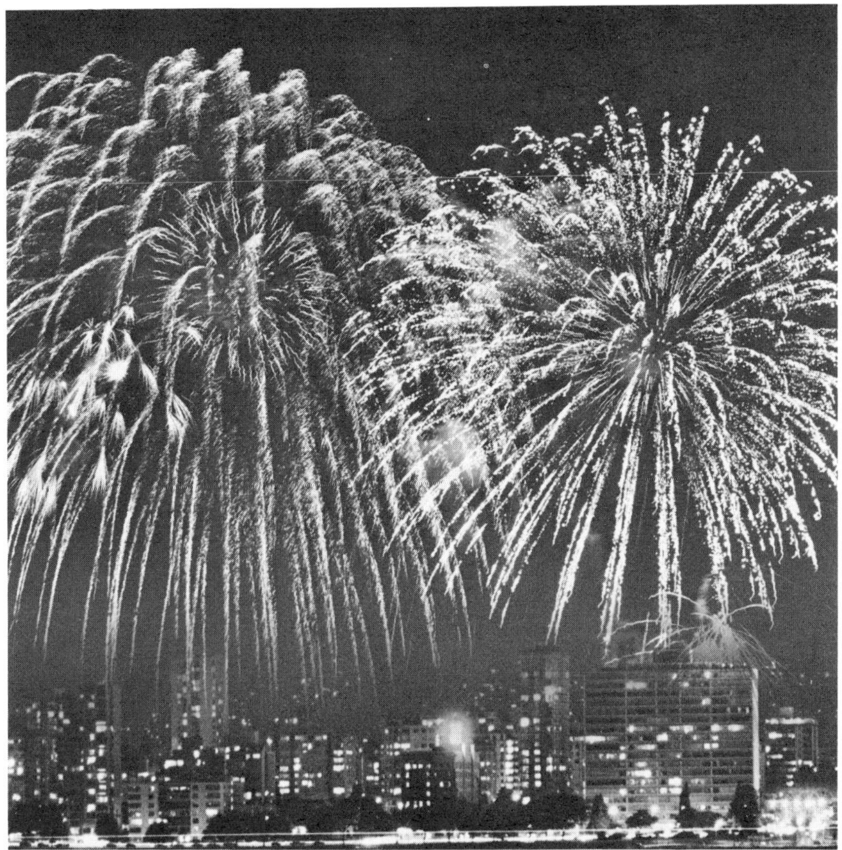

Photo Credit: Kim Yip

Chapter Seventeen—Publishing Your Own Postcards And Greeting Cards

Where The Markets Are

Almost every business in your community is a potential market for a postcard. The corner gas station, the motel down the road, the shopping center and the town bank all are prime targets. Usually a sharp clean picture of their place of business is all that is required.

In this field the photographer must be more of a businessman than a photographer since this is primarily a selling job. The small business owner who has never used postcards as an advertising device is prone to cast a wary eye on what he may consider to be an expensive venture, out of reach of his pocketbook. In reality, postcards in color are relatively inexpensive. This is a major selling point.

While any local printer can print quantity orders of cards, there are houses that specialize in this kind of work and whose prices make it possible for you to quote a low price to your customer and still make a profit. Since all you need do is shoot *one* roll of transparencies which serve as proofs for the client, the time you spend on a job is minimal. One of the large printing firms in the East that specializes in color cards, brochures (more about this), and leaflets is DEXTER PRESS in Springfield, Michigan. They will furnish to the beginning photographer a sample book that contains reproductions of the cards and brochures they print, order forms, suggestions for selling, suggested prices to charge, and commissions that can be earned by the photographer. The cost of the sample book is only a few dollars and is a *must* for the photographer interested in this field. Dexter Press offers a range of services which range from spotting to putting blue skies into your picture.

Don't Stop At Just The Card

Selling a postcard order to the client should be the beginning of your sales efforts. Is the customer a restaurant owner? If so, sell him pictures for his menus. Does your client run the town service station? Why not suggest that you can supply him with a photograph suitable for a calendar that he can distribute to his customers for the New Year! If you live in a resort area, then you should be selling scenic transparencies for use by the various motel and resort owners. They use postcards for their guests to send home. They use brochures in the off season to attract customers for the *following* season. They might use a calendar. Remember, if this field appeals to you, learn to be a salesman.

How About Your Own Cards?

Publishing and distributing your own greeting cards is probably a lot easier than publishing your own book since the mechanics and details can be handled by one individual. If you have something that you are particularly and personally fond of, simply furnish it with a simple caption, lay out the format in which you would like to see it printed, and take it to your neighborhood printshop. Buy matching envelopes and you're ready for the next and most difficult step, that of distribution. If you live in an area where there is a sizable flow of pedestrian traffic and which has card shops, drugstores, or bookshops, then you have found the place to start selling. Offer the cards on a speculation basis, since very few stores will handle unknown products or photographers. Work out an equitable distribution of sales income and offer to take back any that are not sold in a reasonable period of time. If the subject material is timeless and *not* seasonal, your greeting card has a much better chance for a long life. Since the investment in time and money can be kept low, it is a fertile area in which to earn money and achieve recognition.

Market Guide—

Greeting Cards

Art Source
3 Glenview Dr.
Aurora, ONT.
Canada L3R 4C2

Beauty Way
Box 340
Flagstaff, AZ. 86022

Dexter Press
1949 E. Sunshine
Suite 2-210
Springfield, MI. 65804
1-800-431-1905

Dukane Press
2901 Simms Street
Hollywood, FL. 33020

Dynacolor
1182 N.W. 159th Drive
Miami, FL. 33169

Flashcards, Inc.
781 W. Oakland Park Blvd.
Ft. Lauderdale, FL. 33311

Freedom Greetings
1619 Hanford St.
Levittown, PA. 190571

Intercontinental Greetings, Ltd.
176 Madison Ave.
New York, NY. 10016

Joli Greeting Card, Co.
2520 W. Irving Park Rd.
Chicago, IL. 60618

Koppel Color
153 Central Avenue
Hawthorne, NJ. 07507

Landmark General Corp.
Suite 227
475 Gate Five Road
Sausalito, CA. 94966

Mark I
1733-1755 Irving Park Road
Chicago, IL. 60613

McGrew Color Graphics
1615 Grand Avenue
Kansas City, MI. 64108

MWM Color Press
Washington at Olive
Aurora, MI. 65605

Post Cards

The American Postcard Co.
285 Lafayette St.
New York, NY. 10012

Argonaut Press
RR #1, Box 142
Fairfield, IA. 52556

Arpel Graphics
Box 21522
Santa Barbara, CA. 93121

Paramount Cards
Box 1225
Pawtucket, RI. 02862

Photo/Chronicles, Ltd.
500 West End Ave.
New York, NY. 10024

Sackbut Press
2513 E. Webster
Milwaukee, WI. 53211

The Texas Postcard Co.
Box 708
Plano, TX. 75074

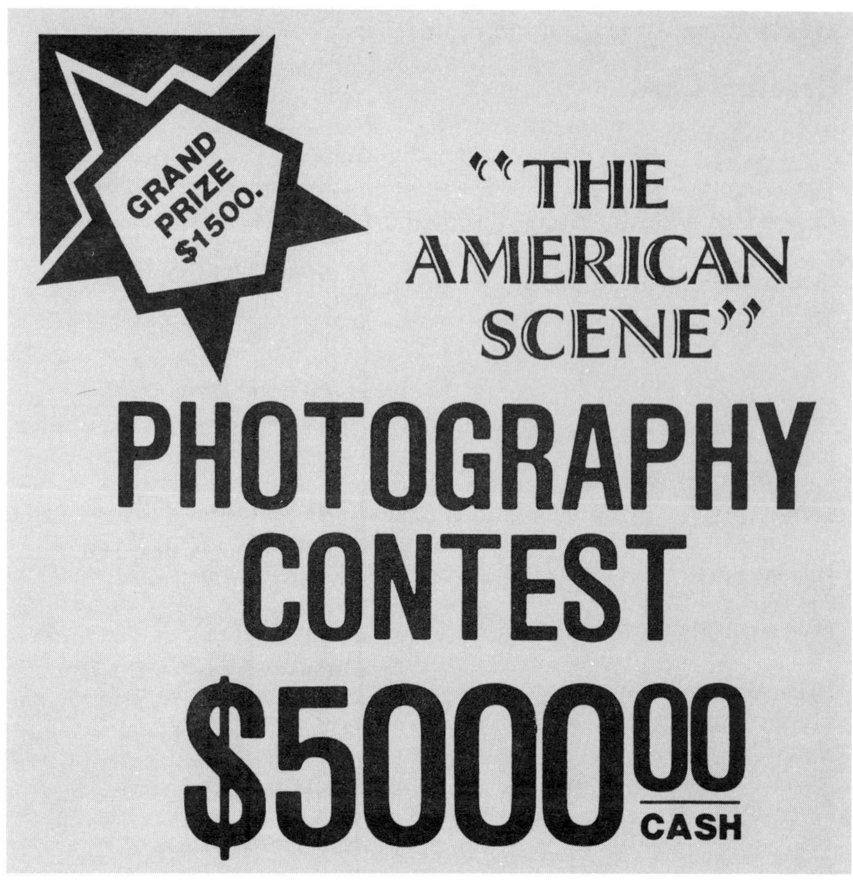

Chapter Eighteen—
More Money With Your Camera

Profits In Photo Contests

Shooting pictures for photo contests is both enjoyable and profitable. Every year thousands and thousands of dollars are paid out by various sponsors of picture contests. While the entries may run into the thousands for some major contests, remember that it takes very little time to print and mail your favorite picture. You may be rewarded with money and prestige for your efforts. Also favorable to the free-lance is the fact that most contests place no restriction on subject matter. There are, of course, those contests that may be limited to cats, dogs, or children (in line with the sponsor's product). Just remember that if you do not enter, you can't possibly win. Since picture contests are well publicized, and closing dates are given months in advance, there is no reason for saying, "I didn't have the time!"

Money In Your Darkroom

Not all photographers enjoy working in the darkroom. While they all enjoy shooting pictures and will go anywhere to take one, the disciplines of the darkroom hold no attraction for some. There is also a large body of photographers who simply do not have the physical facilities to house a darkroom. If you like darkroom work, why not offer yourself as a custom printer? Why not offer to do all the enlarging for both those photographers who hate the darkroom and those amateurs whose interest does not quite go so far as finishing their own prints? Remember, you offer a much better choice than the corner drugstore. You can furnish at reasonable prices hand-made enlargements, cropped and spotted, and still make a good profit. It is not uncommon to earn $10 to $20 an hour doing custom printing and enlarging. If you're good in the darkroom you're worth your weight in gold.

The advantages to you are many. A minimum of equipment is required. The basic darkroom you now have is *all* you need to turn out high-quality prints. Since enlarging is essentially a hand operation that requires skill more than equipment, a good printer can make a first-class print on the cheapest enlarger. Finegrain film developing might be added to the list of services you can offer. Mounting prints for framing is another service that not many photographers have either the time, the patience, or the equipment to tackle. A further advantage of offering custom printing services is that your time is really your own and you can fit your printing schedules into your present job demands. Remember that your services can include both enlarging and custom printing (which is simply the best enlargement you can make). The two services will naturally have different price levels.

Custom enlarging produces the most money in the least amount of time. It is imperative, however, for business reasons and for the building of goodwill, that even those services that do not furnish a high profit level be performed with a smile. Film developing and making contact proof sheets, for instance, are almost "breakeven" kinds of chores, yet they are necessary to the building of a steady clientele. It's something like being the owner of a gas station who washes the customer's windshield and checks the air in his tires, and then watches the car drive off without selling anything. He has performed the goodwill chores that are an essential part of his business.

TYPICAL PRICING SCHEDULE

DEVELOPING

ROLL FILM

35mm or 120	per roll	$ 2.50
	with proof sheet	4.50

Developing to specifications (forced developing), or in special developers, Infra-red & recording film add $2.00

FILM PACK	16 per pack	16.00
	minimum	5.00
CUT FILM		
4x5	per dozen	8.00
	minimum	5.00
8x10	per dozen	12.00
	minimum	8.00

ENLARGEMENTS

FROM SAME NEGATIVE

4x5 or smaller SW/DW (with borders only)

1 to 3 prints	ea. 2.25
4 to 6 prints	ea. 2.10
7 to 12 prints	ea. 1.90

5x7 SW/DW

1 to 3 prints	ea. 2.50
4 to 6 prints	ea. 2.25
7 to 12 prints	ea. 2.00

8x10 SW/DW

1 to 3 prints	ea. 4.00
4 to 6 prints	ea. 3.65
7 to 12 prints	ea. 3.45

LARGE PRINTS

11x14 DW	6.00
14x17 DW	16.00
16x20 DW	14.00
20x24 DW	18.00

CONTACTS AND ENLARGED CONTACTS

CONTACT PROOF SHEETS

35mm or 120 on 8½x11 SW Glossy	2.25
with film developing	4.50

INDIVIDUAL CONTACTS

4x5	SW Glossy	1.50
5x7	SW Glossy	1.75
8x10	SW Glossy	2.10

Prices for larger quantities on request

EXHIBITION PRINTS

UNMOUNTED

8x10	8.00
11x14	18.00
14x17	18.00
16x20	20.00
20x24	30.00
20x30	40.00

CUSTOM COLOR PROCESSING

EKTACHROME

35mm 20 ex. mounted	4.50
35mm 36 ex. mounted	6.95
120/620 rolls in sleeves	4.60
220 rolls in sleeves	9.00

Add $2.00 if film requires developing corrections of ½ or more stops (over or under).

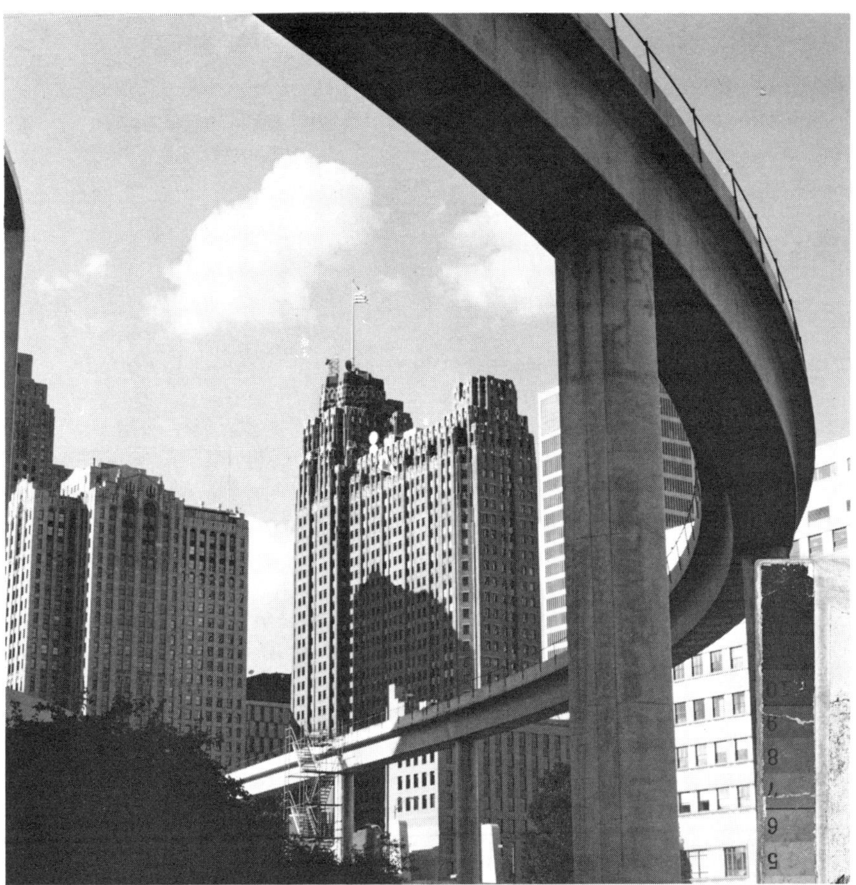

Photo Credit: Kenneth Gust

Chapter Nineteen— The Business Side of Photography

Model Releases

We have stressed throughout this text that photography as practiced by the freelance is a business. The obtaining of model releases wherever necessary is an important part of every picture-taking effort. The model release in its simplest form is an arrangement *in writing* as to what rights the photographer has to the picture in hand. The model's signature will indicate that she or he has given permission to the photographer to use a photograph in whatever manner is agreed in the release. It is *not* necessary that the model be paid for this permission. Model releases may be simple or complicated, depending on the type of photograph involved. The model release does not apply only to the photography of the human face, but in many instances may be required in certain photographs of pets, buildings, brand names, etc. If the content of the photograph is specific in that it identifies a brand or a person (who may own a particular model car, for instance), then a picture of the brand or car *cannot* be published without the owner's consent. *When in doubt, get a model release!* Further, no matter what the nature of the assignment, a model release must be furnished if the person who is paying for the photograph asks for one or when the photograph is to be used for trade publication or advertising.

Keep It Simple

Nothing will frighten away a prospective model more than the appearance of a highly legal and complex-looking release form. Keep your model release as simple as possible without getting too specific. Make it broad enough to give you the right to use the photograph—*period!* Don't be specific. If you get the right to use the picture for one purpose and then discover that you can make another sale in an entirely different area, you may find that the model has moved out of town or has had a change of heart and second thoughts about signing another release. Get everything you need while the transaction is hot! Make copies of the release and retain the original for your files. Use copies when doing business! One final note concerning model releases—minors cannot sign for themselves. In those cases where there is any doubt about the age of a model, make every effort to ascertain whether or not the model is really of legal age. If you do not, the release may be worthless! Remember, a model release is your insurance policy against lawsuits for invasion of privacy.

Here is a sample of a very simple release form.

MODEL RELEASE

I, ______________________________, do hereby acknowledge that for the consideration of __________ I give to the NEW YORK INSTITUTE OF PHOTOGRAPHY full permission to use and reproduce any and all photographs of me taken by ______________________________ ________ on ____________ . These photographs are the property of NEW YORK INSTITUTE OF PHOTOGRAPHY, and may be used in conjunction with my name in any manner in any media, at their discretion.

____
(Signature)

____
(Date)

PLEASE CREDIT

United Press International Photo

This picture is for your publication only and must not be loaded, syndicated or used for advertising purposes without written permission from United Press International. By accepting this picture you agree to hold United Press International harmless from any loss or damage arising by reason of your use or publication of this picture.

UNITED PRESS INTERNATIONAL INC.
220 EAST 42nd STREET
NEW YORK, N.Y. 10017

Chapter Twenty—Picture Rights

Rights—What They Are

When the photographer transmits a print or transparency to a client, he is not selling the paper or film on which the image is reproduced, but rather, selling the right to use that particular image in a manner which is determined at the time of the transaction. Since a good businessman-photographer knows that a single picture may represent more than just one sale, he will try to sell it to as many buyers as possible. In order to do this, he must retain rights to the photograph for as long a time as possible. For instance, he may sell a photograph for *one-time* reproduction to half a dozen different clients. Each client has the right to reproduce that picture once, after which each client has no further right to the picture. The photographer may sell "one-time" publication rights simultaneously to several different buyers—as long as they are non-competitive. The discussion of rights is a complicated and important part of the business aspect of photography and will be discussed in detail in this chapter. Since there are many different arrangements under which a photographer can sell his pictures, the discussion of these rights will be broken down into various segments.

Exclusive Rights

This term is self-explanatory. It means that the photographer is selling all rights to his photograph. Remember that he is *not* selling the photograph itself, but only the right to use it. He may also limit the "exclusive rights" to a specific period of time. He may dictate that these rights are to run for one month or one year, at the end of which time the exclusivity terminates. A photographer may sell exclusive rights in many forms. He may specify that a picture may be used exclusively in an educational text, or on a television program, or that it only be used for domestic consumption and is not to be introduced to any foreign markets. In short, depending upon the photographer and the nature of the picture rights he is selling, he can make any arrangements which suit both his interests and those of his client.

One-Time Rights

As in the example above, a client under this arrangement is permitted to use a photograph *once,* after which the photographer's obligation is discharged and the rights to the picture revert to him.

Book Rights

The photographer gives permission for his picture to be used in a book. Once the book is printed, the rights are once more the photographer's. At the time of signing a contract the photographer should be aware of the fact that since books are revised and reprinted from time to time, he may want to specify that the use of the picture in subsequent publications may entail another payment. This should be written into the original contract.

First Rights

Under this arrangement only those photographs which have never been published before are sold by the photographer. This guarantees the publisher or user of the picture in question that it has never been seen on the printed page or the television screen. Once it has been used, rights revert to the photographer.

All Rights

Without becoming unduly complex, let us state that the phrase *all rights* is essentially the same as *exclusive rights* and that the difference is in those restrictions the photographer himself may want to impose. In a situation where either *all rights* or *exclusive rights* obtains, it is within the right of the user of the photograph to insist that the photographer surrender *permanent* rights to them and that he never offer this picture for sale to anyone else or exhibit or display it in any manner.

Foreign Rights, Language Rights, Promotion Rights

In most instances, a photographer offers domestic use of his product only. In the event that a photograph will be used in another country, he may boost his asking price for *foreign* or *country* rights. *Language rights* obtain when a photograph is to be used in countries that speak the same language. This may take in three or four *different countries.* Price is again negotiable! *Promotion rights* can be sold when a photograph is used in advertising to sell a book or record album. For instance, if a photographer sold a picture for a record cover and that same photograph were to be used in promoting the sales of the record album, then *another* fee would be due the seller of the picture rights. All negotiable, mind you!

Get It Clear And In Writing

More important than using terms like *first rights* or *exclusive rights* or *promotion rights* is to find out exactly what you are selling—at what price—and for what period of time. Spell out in detail the exact terms of the financial arrangements and picture usage. No contract is worth the paper it's written on if the language does not spell out precisely what buyer and seller are entitled to.

Never Sell Your Stock Outright

Photographs are your living. No matter how many rights you sell, or to whom, avoid wherever possible the giving up of *all* rights. In very rare circumstances, and when the financial compensation is far above that which a photographer might receive for usual publication rights, the relinquishing of all rights may be the most profitable way to handle a picture sale. Think about it clearly and carefully. If you decide to surrender all rights to a prize photograph, be sure that you get paid a price in keeping with its value.

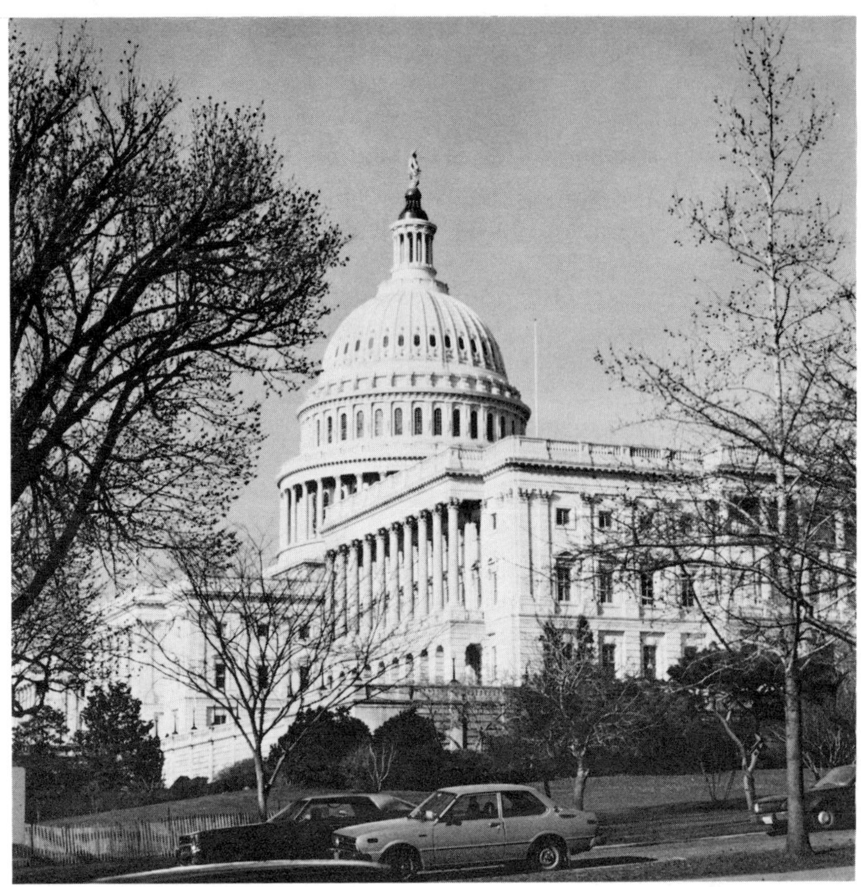

Photo Credit: Tom O. Foster

Chapter Twenty-One—Copyrights

What It Is

A copyright is a legal protection. In the case of a photographer it protects him from the reproduction of any of his copyrighted photographs without his permission.

How To Copyright Your Photographs

Copyright laws have been changed in recent years. In fact, a major revision of the Copyright Act was passed by Congress in January 1978—the first major change in over 50 years! While copyright laws are like legal contracts and need to be studied carefully by a potential user, we will dwell on several important points:

1. The safest way to obtain an ironclad copyright is to file for and secure the copyright before anyone sees the picture, or before it is

published or exhibited in any manner, shape or form. To file for a copyright, write the Register of Copyrights at the Library of Congress, Washington, D.C., 20559. At this writing, *Form VA* and a $10 fee are all that is required.

2. You get substantial temporary protection even before you file for a copyright if you stamp or write the symbol © or the word *Copyright* next to your name on the back of each print. Properly used, the symbol © on your picture, or the word *Copyright*, will give you the necessary legal protections you need pending the submission of the Copyright Notice.

3. In filing with the Registrar of Copyrights, you need a separate form for each photograph, although contact sheets and several prints on one sheet of paper are also acceptable and can be copyrighted for one $10 fee.

4. Do *not* allow the photograph to be published or used in any media unless the word *Copyright* or the symbol © appears in the credit notice printed with the photograph.

5. Don't file for copyright of every single picture you own since at $10 a photograph, you'd soon run out of money. Stamp the © notice on the back of all of them, but save the actual filing for those special pictures that require the extra protection it affords.

More Information

This has been a brief overview of copyrighting. Rather than go deeper into the copyright laws in this text, with the dangers of misinterpretation, we strongly suggest that you write to the *Register of Copyrights, Library of Congress, Washington, D.C. 20559* and ask for the latest copies of copyright statutes. There are several circulars available at this writing, and we list them here for your convenience:

a. *Circular R99*, entitled *Highlights of the New Copyright Law.*
b. *Circular R15a*, entitled *Duration of Copyright Under the New Law.*
   Circular FL107, entitled *Copyrights for Photographs.*
d. There are several others which deal with copyrights for motion pictures (*#45*); Radio and Television (*#47*); and a general booklet, entitled *General Information On Copyright.*
e. Don't forget to request several copies of *Form VA.*

If You Work On Assignment

Insofar as the copyrights to a picture are concerned, bear in mind that the owner usually obtains the copyright. Anything you produce on assignment for a client belongs to the *client* and cannot be copyrighted by the photographer. Become familiar with copyright laws.

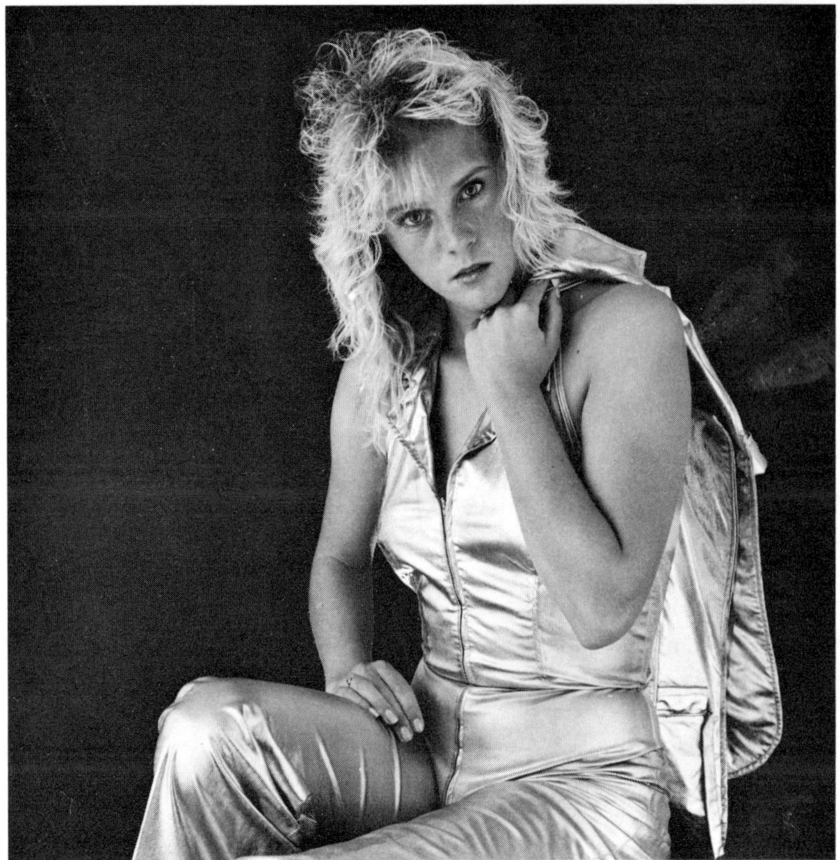

Photo Credit: Patricia A. Powers

Chapter Twenty-Two— More About The Business Side

Should You Have a "Rep"?

In the jargon of the photographer, a "rep" is a representative or salesperson-someone who goes out knocking on clients' doors in an effort to sell your services. If you are the kind of photographer who works constantly, producing many salable pictures, the "rep" may mean the difference between success and failure for you. Of course, reps can function on many levels. A good friend who knows lots of people can function as an unpaid rep and bring in some business. Much more business-like, of course, is the payment of a commission to someone who is qualified by training and temperament to sell your wares.

Preparing A Portfolio

Just as the good salesman is never without his sample case, so the photographer who calls on a client is never without his "book," a portfolio of sample pictures. The book should be fluid and flexible, with pictures being changed constantly and with selected photographs aimed at particular clients. Remember, if a client is in the hardware business, it is highly unlikely that he will be interested in your flower portfolio! The art director for a company that manufactures beauty products wants to see a portfolio showing how you handle perfume, colognes, soaps. Use your head. Show the picture buyer what he wants to see. Telling him that you're great is not going to impress him. Showing him successful pictures you may have made for similar clients will.

How To Build Your Portfolio Gradually

If you're good behind the camera, you may be able to construct an adequate beginning portfolio by photographing products in your studio. If you can handle lighting and arrangement and show just a little bit of imagination, most picture buyers will give you a chance at a job. Depending on the kind of work you specialize in, it is possible over a short period of time to put together portfolios of sports pictures, human interest essays, casual business portraits, models, how-to pictures, industrial shots, and possibly several photographs using various lenses in which imagination has been matched to mechanics. There will be many times when your assignment may call for a variety of pictures, and it is a good idea to be able to display a well-rounded talent. For instance, in the average annual report, you may be required to make a formal portrait of an executive at his desk, a photograph of a worker at a milling lathe, and an overall view of the plant buildings, showing how they blend into the surrounding environment. On this sort of assignment, the pictures that go into the portfolio must be carefully selected. Use your judgment.

How Many Pictures Do You Need?

This is probably the most difficult question to answer. A portfolio should be big enough to give the client an idea of your talents, yet not so big that it puts him to sleep. A dozen or so powerful images make a much deeper impression than 30 or 40 so-so pictures. Don't throw everything you own into your portfolio just for the sake of numbers.

What's Best—Prints Or Transparencies?

This is a question that usually answers itself. If you shoot only black-and-white, then the 8x10 print is the universally accepted size. If you shoot color (and you probably will), then the question of the best way to present your shots arises. In the case of 35mm transparencies, there are two accepted methods. The first is to carry a projector or viewer. This can become tiring after a while. A much better method is to determine if the client has a projector and, if so, your slides may be carried in separate trays that fit the client's projector. An alternate method is to put slides in transparent acetate pages that are punched for 3-ring binders. These make for fairly easy viewing over a light box and permit the photographer to carry several pages of 20 transparencies each on those occasions where he has two or more appointments in the same day. Of course, larger sheet-film sizes can be handled in a similar manner. 4x5 or larger transparencies may be placed into individual sleeves and shown one at a time like prints. For better protection against fingerprints and corner damage, the slide in its protective sleeve may be taped to an 8x10 mount with a window cut in the center. In this manner, the transparency is viewed by holding the edge of the cardboard mount rather than the acetate sleeve directly. There may be times when you feel that a good quality color print may do a better job of selling. If so, mount the print on a stiff board to prevent edge damage and spray the surface with a clear protective lacquer to safeguard against smudges and fingerprints.

Clippings And Tearsheets

If you've had the good fortune to have been published prior to visiting a new client, then the most powerful part of your "book" can be *tearsheets.* These are carefully cut out of the publication they appear in, and either originals or copies may be part of the portfolio. They are extremely impressive and are the hallmark of the professional. They indicate that you've made the "big leagues."

Review

1. Black-and-white or color prints are suitable for a portfolio. They should be well made, and either laminated or mounted to boards for maximum protection.

2. Acetate sleeves, pages designed to hold 35mm slides, and slide projectors or viewers are all acceptable for portfolio use. Where the client has a projector, carry slides in a tray that is compatible with his machine.

3. Don't overload your presentation. Show him only the best you have and show him what he wants to see.

4. Shoot pictures for your portfolio at every opportunity. It takes time to build a book with enough variety to cover any assignment you may be called on to do.

5. Be an editor. Before you visit a prospective client, pay a lot of attention to the material you are going to show him. If you are in doubt about a particular picture or slide, leave it home! Above all—use your head.

Keeping A Negative File

The moment you begin producing pictures on a steady basis, the setting up of a system of identification and easy retrieval is imperative. If it takes you two days to find the slide of the Hopi Indian you photographed on your last Western trip, you're headed for trouble.

Systems You Can Try

The method of filing negatives is not really important as long as the system you choose works for you. 35mm negatives are usually kept in acetate sleeves which are numbered in India ink or Magic Marker. If a photographer shoots essays as his primary output, he may elect to identify a whole job with code letters for the essay, and then number each negative sequentially. For instance, an essay on a day in the life of a suburban housewife may be identified as *Wife-1*, *Wife-2*, or *H* (for *Housewife*) followed by the frame number. The date of the shooting may also be included. After contact sheets are made, they should be marked to correspond with each matching roll of film, and may be filed in a three-ring binder or in a box. Again, this is not important. What is important is that you set up a system that is easy for you to understand and which permits you to find the negatives you need when you need them. Once a negative is numbered with a particular set of code letters, those letters should never be used again for any other job. A register may also be used to list jobs done, clients name and date of shooting. This may be broken down even further by using subject matter or geographical locations as the prime headings. For instance, the slides you took of those Hopi Indians may be listed in your register under *Indians*. When you have reason to retrieve the negative or transparency, the register will also tell you in what file or box the material is stored. The numbers you used on your negatives and contact sheets should always appear on any duplicates you may send out so that when they come back to you they can be easily filed where they belong.

Breaking Down The Categories

One of the most popular filing systems resembles that used by many stock picture agencies. The primary identification is by subject matter. You may use both primary and secondary categories, such as *Children (at play)*, *Children (with adults)*, *Children (with pets)*. Note that the primary classification of *Children* is further identified by a secondary category. Your file on children might thus be broken down into a dozen different divisions. If you shoot three or four rolls of film on the same subject, then each roll of film should be identified with a separate numeral following the regular coding sequence. For instance, you may have identified a job as *IN-6-80*, meaning *Indians, June, 1980*. If you shot more than one roll your coding would be *IN-6-80-1* (for the first roll) and then *-2, -3, -4* for subsequent rolls. In identifying prints, you may choose to also include the frame number. Thus, a print might be designated *IN-6-80-1-17*, signifying frame 17.

Filing Your Negatives And Prints

While some common methods of filing involve the taping of negative sleeves to the backs of their respective contact sheets, this system proves to be unwieldy in that a bulky sandwich results. The much preferred method is to file prints and negatives separately. Contact sheets may be conveniently stored in three ring binders, and negative sleeves (properly marked on the outside) stored in boxes, file cabinets, or 3-ring binders—whichever is most convenient. When a particular print is required, the contact sheet file is consulted, the number noted, and the negatives then retrieved from the negative file.

Filing Transparencies

There are several workable filing systems available for transparencies. The system which works best for you really depends on how many transparencies you own. If you do not have too many, the boxes in which you receive them back from the processor can be marked with the job number or description and filed away as is. The chances are that you'll want something more structured and permanent. Three-ring binders with acetate pages holding 20 transparencies each, make for easy perusal and retrieval of particular slides. Metal file boxes are available that will hold several hundred slides and have a printed log for recording numbers of each transparency and subject matter. Depending on the kind of subject matter you shoot, you may find the *Carousel* type tray the best method of all. Since you will probably have occasion to show slides to clients with increasing frequency, it makes good sense to store the slides in a tray which doubles both as file and portfolio of sorts. Whichever method you choose, don't forget the basic rules about segregating slides according to subject matter and code number. The best system is that which permits you to easily locate the slide you need with the least amount of trouble.

In Conclusion

In the preparation of this text the authors have tried to present basic facts. They have avoided the use of extraneous material or "fillers" for the sake of making the text impressively oversize. Market listings have been checked so that up-to-the-minute information is presented. Perhaps most important, all of this information is meant to serve as an *introduction* to the training you will receive in your NYI Course. You can't possibly succeed as a freelance unless your skills as a photographer are at the highest professional level. That's the level at which your NYI Course is going to have you aim. That's the level at which you will operate...if you apply yourself to your NYI training with diligence, seriousness, and enthusiasm. With these attitudes, you can only succeed!

Fine Art Photography

Art Now/USA, The National Art Museum and Gallery Guide
320 Bonnie Burn Road
PO Box 219
Scotch Plains, NJ. 07076

Photography Galleries and Selected Museums: A Survey and Directory
533 Rialto
Venice, CA. 90291

Photo Magazines

American Photographer Magazine
485 5th Avenue
New York, NY. 10036

Modern Photography
ABC Leisure Magazines
825 7th Avenue
New York, NY. 10019

Industrial Photography
475 Park Avenue South
New York, NY. 10016

Petersen's PhotoGraphic
6725 Sunset Blvd.
Los Angeles, CA. 90028

Photo Communique
PO Box 299
Buffalo, NY. 14222

Photo/Design Magazine
1 Bridge Plaza
Ft. Lee, NJ. 07024
(201) 944-8200

Photo District News
167 3rd Avenue
New York, NJ. 10003
(212) 677-8418

Popular Photography
1 Park Avenue
New York, NY. 10016

Photo Newsletters

Aperture
20 E. 23rd Street
New York, NY. 10010
(212) 505-5555

Rangefinder
Box 1703
1312 Lincoln Blvd.
Santa Monica, CA. 90406

Photoletter
Photo Search, Int'l
Osceola, WI. 54020

Moneygram: A Market for Every Photo
1768 Rockville Drive
Baldwin, NY. 11510

Photo Societies

A.S.M.P. (American Society of Magazine Photographers)
205 Lexington Avenue
New York, NY. 10016
(212) 899-9144

Professional Photographers of America
1090 Executive Way
Des Plaines, IL. 60018

Professional Women Photographers
43 W. 22nd Street
New York, NY. 10010
(212) 255-9678

Photo Trade Shows

Conference of Professional Photographers
17 Washington Street
Box 4990
Norwalk, CT. 06856

Photographic Society of America Regional Conventions
2005 Walnut Street
Philadelphia, PA. 19041

Visual Communications Congress
Media Horizons, Inc.
50 W. 23 St.
New York, NY. 10010